THE MUTUAL SOCIETY

The Beckly Social Service Lecture, 1962

THE MUTUAL SOCIETY

Aspects of the Relationship of Men and Women

by

KENNETH G. GREET

WIPF & STOCK · Eugene, Oregon

Wipf and Stock Publishers
199 W 8th Ave, Suite 3
Eugene, OR 97401

The Mutual Society
Aspects of the Relationship of Men and Women
By Greet, Kenneth G.
ISBN 13: 978-1-5326-3066-8
Publication date 4/6/2017
Previously published by Epworth Press, 1962

Every effort has been made to trace the current copyright
owner of this publication but without success. If you have
any information or interest in the copyright, please contact the publishers.

CONTENTS

	INTRODUCTION	1
1	HISTORY OF A HERESY	5
2	VARIATIONS ON A THEME	24
3	A TRUMPET VOICE SOUNDS	44
4	MELTING MORALITY?	68
5	EFFECTS OF AN EXPLOSION	92
6	SCIENTIFIC INVASION	116
7	INTERLUDE FOR THEOLOGY	140
8	PROGRESS IN PARTNERSHIP	160
	INDEX	169

INTRODUCTION

THE THEME of this lecture is the rise and development of 'the mutual society'. This phrase, which, of course, occurs in the Order of Service for Christian Marriage, is here lifted out of its narrower context and used to describe an order, still in the process of creation, in which men and women have re-examined their traditional roles, adjusted themselves to a new understanding of the truth that men and women are equal, and seen more deeply into the significance of sex itself.

In the perspective of history it may well appear that the most revolutionary fact in this very remarkable century was the advance of women from a position of supposed inferiority and actual subordination to one of equality with men. At the present time, however, we are still grappling with the results of the impact of this continuing revolution, some of them beneficial, others of less doubtful value. The revolution itself is the result of many interrelated factors, and affects the life of the individual and society in a multiplicity of ways. One of its most important aspects is the spirit of inquiry which it has released. A new kind of question is being asked. It is increasingly recognized that there is a deceptive simplicity about the phrase 'the equality of the sexes'. We now have to ask what this equality means in terms of personal and social relationship. Men and women are asking questions about themselves and about each other that were not and could not be asked before the great revolution which began to free women from the shackles of subordination, and equally to liberate men for the adventure of a full human relationship with the opposite sex. Inevitably, and in many respects encouragingly, the searchlight of enquiry is turned on the nature and meaning of sex itself.

It would be difficult to exaggerate the influence upon Western culture of the teaching of the Christian Church about sexual matters. Some aspects of that teaching are under heavy fire at the present time. There is urgent need for a reasoned Christian defence of all that is valid in our tradition, but an equally pressing necessity for a clear repudiation of what is seen to be false. Whilst there is a great deal of literature on the physical aspects of sex and marriage, and the Marriage Guidance Movement is producing some useful material to help the marriage counsellor, there are fewer books dealing, from the Christian standpoint, with the other and wider aspects of human sexuality. The Department on the Co-operation of Men and Women in Church and Society of the World Council of Churches has produced some useful reports, but the channels of ecumenical communication have not yet been sufficiently well dug for these to reach the man in the pew. Some provision has been made for the serious student. Notably, in this country, Dr D. Sherwin Bailey has written an admirable and scholarly treatise, *The Man-Woman Relation in Christian Thought*;[1] while in America, Dr W. G. Cole has in two books examined interpretations of sex in Christianity, and the practices and teachings of the Old and New Testaments.[2]

There is need, however, for the rather less specialized treatment of the subject which will promote its discussion on sound lines at the level of the local fellowship group in church and parish.

The purpose of this lecture is to encourage the ordinary enquiring Christian to ask the right questions, or at least some of them, and, where possible, to discover the answers.

---

[1] Published by Longmans, 1959.
[2] *Sex in Christianity and Psychoanalysis* (Allen & Unwin, 1956); *Sex and Love in the Bible* (Hodder & Stoughton, 1960).

Our discussion must begin with the fundamental question, 'What was the mind and purpose of God in creating half of us men and the other half women?' It is later suggested that in the past the answer to that question has been too much limited to merely biological considerations connected with the propagation of the human species. A number of factors now compel us to examine this question in a wider context and to look for the answer in terms of the creation of a mutual society in which men and women are complementary. Our understanding of what this means, or could mean, is hindered by those persistent errors which have for countless centuries impoverished the relations of men and women, both within the narrow focus of marriage and in the wider life of the community. Chief among these are the hoary heresies that there is something inherently sinful about the physical manifestations of human sexuality, and, linked with this, the idea that women are inferior and subordinate to men.

In order to assist our understanding of the questions raised by a consideration of the mutual society the lecture begins with a brief examination of the characteristic emphases of biblical teaching about the relationship of men and women, and of the influences that helped to shape the early tradition. The positive naturalism of the Hebrew outlook is noted, but also the negative influences which formed the seed-bed of the disastrous heresies referred to in the previous paragraph.

The second chapter traces the development of the tradition in the centuries during which the Christian gospel spread across the world. Although that tradition altered under the influence of events and the thinking of successive generations, the negative influences persisted in a pattern which remained virtually unchallenged until comparatively recent times.

In the modern era a number of factors have combined

to undermine certain aspects of Christian traditional teaching on the subject of sex. The most powerful of these factors are: the emancipation of women; the change in the moral climate to which modern psychology and its related disciplines have contributed; the effects of the population explosion; and the spectacular invasion of science into realms hitherto regarded as God's prerogative. A brief examination of each of these factors is attempted in Chapters 3-6, and some indication is given of the kind of response which Christians are making to the challenge they present. Chapter 7 shows the importance of theology and the relevance of Christian doctrine for a right understanding of the meaning and purpose of sex. The final chapter suggests certain practical steps which the Church must take if it is to encourage true progress in partnership between the sexes.

Although there are very real difficulties and dangers in the present situation, there are also exciting new possibilities of creating a society in which men and women live and work together with a degree of mutual understanding never widely achieved before. If Christians are to play their part in accelerating progress in partnership between the sexes they must be willing consciously to descend into the arena of the ongoing revolution of our times, and not to stand as timid spectators of a struggle they do not understand, limiting their contribution in the main to moralistic warnings and condemnatory clichés. And if sometimes that arena of conflict is an uncomfortable and confusing place we may dare to believe that it is better to arrive in heaven dirty with the dust of battle than clad in the clean clothes of decent but devilish detachment from the world's great need.

CHAPTER ONE

HISTORY OF A HERESY

IN DECEMBER 1936, following the abdication of King Edward VIII, Archbishop Lang appealed over the radio for 'a return to religion and to the standards of morality laid down by our fathers'. Such appeals are not infrequently made by Christians when they are confronted with the facts about divorce, or the illegitimate birth-rate, or the increase in sexual crimes. It must be admitted, however, that there are aspects of the teaching of our fathers in the faith to which no sensible person would want to return. The traditional views of the Church on sexual matters form a strange patchwork. We shall only see clearly our present obligations if we subject that tradition to critical examination in the light of our contemporary knowledge and experience and the insights they afford.

Such an examination is bound to reveal the distressingly negative character of part of the Church's teaching, but it ought not to blind us to the positive achievements of the Church in preserving much that is of supreme value in the face of very strong influences emanating from rival religions and philosophies. It is sometimes suggested that the influence of the Christian tradition on sexual thought and behaviour has been an unmitigated disaster. The apostle Paul, in particular, is often castigated for the part he is alleged to have played in the destruction of human happiness caused by the imposition of a negative and guilt-laden attitude to sexual matters. One writer, in a book on *The Feminine Character* claims that the emancipation of women was 'made possible by the relaxation of the hold which the Christian churches had for centuries exercised over people's minds'.[1] Such sweeping generalizations reveal a lack of historical perspective and an absence of sympathetic appreciation which obscure vital aspects of the truth.

A balanced judgement about the Christian interpretation of sex must take into account the sort of world into which Jesus was born and the influences which affected the thought and outlook of the first Christians. It is necessary first of all to look briefly at the attitudes and practices of the Hebrews (as revealed in the Old Testament), the Greeks, the Romans, and the Orientals; then at the teaching of Jesus and Paul in the New Testament. Our main concern will be with the approach to sexuality itself and with the various ideas about the relative status of men and women.

THE HEBREWS

Most students of biblical history are familiar with the suggestion that it was odd of God to choose the Jews. In many ways, however, it was not odd at all. For one thing, since the climax of His redemptive plan was to be the incarnation of His Blessed Son, what better than that Jesus should come to a people well-schooled in the sacramental view which sees in the material the vehicle of the spiritual? It is one of the profoundly important characteristics of Hebrew thought that it is unashamedly naturalistic. 'The earth is the LORD's, and the fulness thereof' (Ps 24[1]). In the first chapter of Genesis we are told that 'God saw every thing that He had made, and, behold, it was very good' (verse 31). The God who has created the heavens and the earth reveals His glory to men through the works of His hands. 'The heavens declare the glory of God; and the firmament sheweth his

[1] Viola Klein (Kegan Paul, 1946), p. 17.

handywork'. (Ps 19¹). Such are the characteristic notes of the Old Testament when in song and speech it celebrates the God of all creation.

It is not surprising that the Song of Songs found its place in the Canon of the Hebrew Scriptures. In that collection of lyrical verses the parts of the human body are described in poetry that is void of prudery, and its eight short chapters are unshadowed by the sense of shame which brought a later generation to believe that the way of holiness lay in the mortifying of the flesh. It is, perhaps, a little amusing to reflect that the two ideas which enabled the Song of Songs to gain a place in the Canon of Hebrew Scripture were that its author was King Solomon and that its language symbolized the relation of Jehovah with his people. Neither of these ideas is tenable today. In fact, it never mentions the name of Jehovah and contains no word of prayer or praise. Later generations of Christians, who managed to spare their blushes by interpreting the Song allegorically as referring to the relation of Christ with His church, may be complimented on their ingenuity but scarcely on their common sense. The Book stands as a welcome testimony to an attitude of glad acceptance of the beauty of physical sexuality. One imagines that this is the attitude which D. H. Lawrence was trying to recapture in some of his novels, though this is not the place to embark upon an assessment of the degree to which he succeeded or failed.

Although it is often asserted that the Genesis story of creation shows that the original sin of Adam and Eve was sexual, a careful examination of the narrative shows that this is not so. What the serpent said to Eve about the forbidden fruit was: 'In the day ye eat thereof, then your eyes shall be opened, and ye shall be as God' (Gen 3⁵). The essence of their sin was the pride of self-centredness which usurps the place of God. The infection of this sin spreads to every aspect of man's life, and its effect upon sexual relationship is seen in the sense of shame signified by the aprons of fig-leaves with which they covered their nakedness.

The stern condemnation of irregular sexual behaviour in the Old Testament is not due to any deeply rooted fear of physical sexuality, but rather is the result of a high ideal of family life and a profound respect for the personality of each individual. The Old Testament leaves us in no doubt that marriage was favourably regarded by the Jewish people, though the reason for this lies more in the fact that it was the means of propagating the Elect People than that it was a supreme form of personal relationship exemplifying human fellowship at its richest and most creative level. The corollary of this is the repeated reference to singleness or barrenness as a reproach. The blessing of Abraham whose seed shall be numerous 'as the stars of the heaven' (Gen 22^{17}) may be contrasted with the remark of Rachel when eventually she conceives a child: 'God hath taken away my reproach' (Gen 30^{23}).

Unhappily, however, a positive attitude towards sex and family relationship did not lead to any significant questioning of the patriarchal pattern which assumed the superior and dominant role of the man. It is true, of course, that there is abundant evidence in the Old Testament that women played a not unimportant role in the religious observances of the Hebrew people. The code of Deuteronomy provides for the presence of women at the Temple festivals.[2] Women served at the door of the tent of meeting.[3] Various women appear in the history of Israel as prophetesses, as, for example, Deborah.[4] But both in the realm of religion and in the life of society it was assumed that women were meant to be subservient to men and this assumption was reinforced by the myth of

---

[2] *See* Deuteronomy 5^{18}.   [3] *See* Exodus 38^8.   [4] *See* Judges 4^{4-5}.

the creation of Woman out of a rib taken from the side of the first Man while he slept.

THE GREEKS

The history of sexual habits and ideas in Greek civilization is a story of strange contrasts. In pre-Homeric times the worship of a great mother goddess seems to have produced a kind of matriarchy. The legend of the Amazons, which was regarded by the Greeks as describing their own early history, refers to the women warriors who burned off their breasts—the word '*a-mazone*' means 'without breasts'. They thus were supposed to have rendered themselves fit to bear arms in battle. Later, however, the male gods of Mount Olympus mastered the goddesses, though the Greeks continued to worship the feminine principle embodied in their deities.

One of the results of this is that the sexual differences between men and women are played down. Often it is difficult to distinguish between male and female Greek statues. In Plato's *Symposium* Aristophanes declares that originally the two sexes were united in one body which was rent in two as a punishment for sin. This is very different from the biblical account of the origin of human sexuality, and it is not difficult to see why homosexual practices played such a significant part in the pattern of behaviour among the Greeks. The stern and searing words of St Paul in the opening chapter of the Epistle to the Romans are directed against these practices.

During the later Hellenistic period of Greek culture sexual thought is very greatly affected by the influence of the Oriental mystery religions, as we shall see in a moment.

The worship of the masculine form is only one aspect of the subordination of womanhood that followed the eclipse of the matriarchy. The doctrine of male arrogance is well to the fore in the philosophy of Aristotle, whose arguments and alleged evidence about the inferiority of women have been employed by ignorant people ever since.

THE ROMANS

In contrast with the Greeks, the Romans emphasized the differences between the sexes. Indeed they appear to have invented the much-abused word 'sex', for *sexus*, meaning the difference between male and female, derives from the Latin verb *secare*, to cut or sever. A full sex life for both men and women was regarded as both natural and necessary.

In early Rome the power of the male head over his household was supreme. As one finds in some of the younger countries in Africa today, however, as simple agriculture was replaced by a more complicated economy, the pattern altered. A wife became less of an economic asset and more of a liability. So the familiar bride-price paid by the husband was replaced by a dowry paid to the husband. Later this was paid direct to the wife, and she had the right to take it with her if she left her husband's household. This growing independence, strengthened by the right of the wife to divorce her husband on sufficient grounds, did not, however, make for a more stable society. It is always difficult in seeking to assess the moral state of a nation not to distort the picture by putting too much emphasis on the spectacular sins which hit the headlines. But there is a great deal of evidence to show that, while there were doubtless very many who lived a family life of exemplary quality, prostitution flourished and pornography was rife in the Roman world into which the Christian gospel first came.

THE ORIENTALS

One of the lessons of history is that there is always a two-way traffic on the road of the conqueror. This is true whether he is a military commander intent upon building an Empire or a modern missionary concerned to bring all men into submission to Christ. When people meet in battle or in fellowship they leave their mark upon each other. So when Alexander the Great sought to bring the benefits of Hellenistic culture to the superstitious Orient he exposed the Western world, albeit unwittingly, to the religious influences of men who had turned their backs on the world of matter, seeking a spiritual salvation by escape from its trammels.

The Gnostic philosophy was characterized by just such a contempt for things material, and was especially suspicious of the body. At one extreme were the Gnostics who extolled virginity and denounced marriage as an inferior and sinful state. Opposed to them were the libertines who held that the 'spiritual' man could do what he liked, since material actions were of no account. This is Oriental dualism in its most obtuse and mischievous form. It is an outlook and a belief which profoundly and increasingly influenced the thinking of later generations of Christians.

In glancing at the varying traditions which combined to form the environment of the early Church we have noticed several emphases which affected the thought and viewpoint of the Christian Church on sexual matters. There is what has been described as the naturalism of the Hebrew people whose influence was paramount, because Jesus was 'great David's greater Son', and the Jewish tradition was the seedbed of the Christian religion. The Greeks and Romans contributed in their distinctive ways to the muddled sexual morality and the excesses against which the early Church had to take so firm a stand. The dualism of the Oriental world began to permeate men's minds in the Hellenistic period and many mistook the road of escape for the highway of salvation. Finally we have observed that, whilst at times the status of women was elevated above that of men, the predominating pattern in all four cultures was that of male leadership and female subordination.

We may now enquire what was distinctive in the Christian teaching about sexual relationship, and how far that teaching was coloured by current philosophies.

JESUS

Those who look in the New Testament for a new code of sexual morality will look in vain. The distinctively Christian contribution is a doctrine of Man which emphasizes the importance of respecting the personality of others, and the promise of God-given power which can transform both Man and society.

In considering the bearing of the life and teaching of Jesus on the matter of sexual relationship we have to rely more upon general inferences than upon the quotation of proof texts. Although there is a stern and demanding note in the teaching of our Lord, of which His words about divorce are an example,[5] there is an almost complete absence of the asceticism which later became a dominant feature of the Christian tradition.

He quoted with approval from the Book of Genesis: ' "Have you never read that the Creator made them from the beginning male and female?"; and he added, "For this reason a man shall leave his father and mother, and be made one with his wife; and the two shall become one flesh?" ' (Mt 19^{4-5}) He 'sanctioned and adorned' the wedding at Cana in Galilee and His parables are full of references to family life.

It has been suggested that the concluding verses of the second of the Matthean passages on divorce betray a dualistic emphasis. The disciples' response to what Jesus

---

[5] *See* Mark 10^{2-12}; Luke 16^{18}, and Matthew 5^{27-30} and 19^{1-12}.

has said about the binding nature of the marriage vows is, 'If that is the position with husband and wife, it is better to refrain from marriage' (Mt 19¹⁰). To this Jesus replies: 'That is something which not everyone can accept, but only those for whom God has appointed it. For while some are incapable of marriage because they were born so, or were made so by men, there are others who have themselves renounced marriage for the sake of the kingdom of Heaven. Let those accept it who can' (Mt 19¹¹⁻¹²). This passage, however, is really one of several in which our Lord insists that men must seek the Kingdom of God *first*. Marriage or family are certainly not evil in themselves but are only to be forsworn if they become the ultimate end of a man's life, usurping the place of God and hindering the pursuit of His purposes.

Another New Testament passage which might seem to have a dualistic emphasis is the one recorded by all three synoptic writers in which Jesus answers a question from the Sadducees by saying: 'At the resurrection men and women do not marry, but are like angels in heaven' (Mt 22³⁰; Mk 12²⁵, Lk 20³⁵⁻⁶). It must be remembered, however, that when Jesus spoke of the resurrection He was using the term in the Jewish sense which implied the resurrection of the body—an idea quite inconsistent with dualism. He is here looking forward to that future life in which the pattern of our existence will be different, but He is not in any way condemning the present order.

One of the most graphic and moving passages in the New Testament is the account of the woman caught in an act of adultery (Jn 8¹⁻¹¹). Although most of the ancient authorities omit this story, it is entirely consistent with the attitude of Jesus reflected in other parts of the gospels. When he refuses to condemn the woman, telling her to go and sin no more, our Lord displays an approach to those found guilty of sexual sin which contrasts vividly with the censorious and vindictive spirit of those whose synthetic anger is merely a thin disguise for their own sense of guilt. In this incident Jesus shows clearly that His attitude to sex is that of Hebrew naturalism rather than that of Hellenistic dualism.

There are, of course, two facts about our Lord which have influenced Christian thought on the subject of sex and have, unhappily, been called in evidence by those who have subscribed to the morbid view that venereal sexuality is inherently evil. One is the fact that Jesus did not marry. It belongs to the realities of the case that there can be no positive answer to the question: 'Why did Jesus never marry?' The incarnation of the Son of God was a unique event. When human comment and explanation have done their best to expound the meaning of the Divine Visitation there must necessarily remain much that is mysterious and beyond the reach of our understanding, unless the great design of God is to be reduced to the compass of an earthly scheme. One obvious point is that the very fact of incarnation involved God in 'the scandal of particularity'. Just as Jesus had to be born as a member of one race, speaking the native language of His own people, so He had to be born either as a boy or a girl. Those who argue that no man could be the Saviour of the whole race, since half of humanity is female, are making sweeping and unargued assumptions. Perhaps the best rejoinder to this strange assertion is that it all depends upon the man. If the man in question is indeed the Son of God then we are immediately face to face with the activity of God, to whom all good things are possible. We shall deal more fully with this point in Chapter 7. What is surely indefensible is to regard the celibacy of Jesus as an argument against marriage. As we have seen, the denigration of marriage finds no support in the teaching of our Lord. It is reasonable to suggest that our own view should be based on clear teaching rather than on dubious interpretations of the inescapably mysterious mechanism of incarnation whereby we see

> *Our God contracted to a span,*
> *Incomprehensibly made man.*

The other fact about our Lord which has been mischievously employed by those with unhealthy views about sex is that He was born of a virgin. This has been taken to imply that the normal means of generation is inherently sinful otherwise God would not have rejected it in favour of a so-called immaculate conception by the Holy Ghost (See the next Chapter, p. 36.) It may well be that it is reluctance to accept the idea of God's unwillingness to use the normal means of procreation, rather than doubts about its historicity or inability to believe in the miraculous, which has caused some Christians to reject the doctrine of the Virgin Birth. Surely, however, we are under no compulsion to believe that because God uses one method He thereby condemns another. However true it may be that sin has sullied sexual relationship, as it has spoiled every other aspect of life, the fact remains that coition between man and woman is the original means devised by God for the propagation of children. Reading into the minds of others thoughts that are not there is one of the devil's most ancient ways of making mischief. This is particularly true when he entices us into putting into the mind of God thoughts that have festered in our own diseased imaginations.

When we turn to the attitude of Jesus towards women we find the same positive and natural approach. The Fourth Gospel records the conversation Jesus had with a Samaritan woman at Jacob's Well (Jn 4^{7-27}), and also refers to the surprise of the disciples, occasioned no doubt partly by the fact that our Lord talked so freely with a

Samaritan, but also by His treating a woman with as much consideration as if she had been a man. 'At that moment his disciples returned, and were astonished to find him talking with a woman!' (Jn 4^{27}).

St Luke, who refers especially to the place occupied by women in the gospel story, tells us that there were a number who helped Jesus during His ministry. They included Mary Magdalene, Joanna the wife of Chuza who was Herod's steward, and Susanna (Lk 8$^{2-3}$). Women, too, played an important part in the drama of the Vigil of Calvary, and the Resurrection. It is true that no women were included in the band of twelve Apostles, and presumably also the seventy (Lk 10^{1}) who were sent out in pairs to the towns and villages which Jesus was intending to visit were an all-male company. No conclusion, however, can be drawn from that which would be valid in the changed social conditions of our day.

In the life and teaching of Jesus, then, we find no support either for the repudiation or suspicion of sex which characterized the attitude of some later Christians, or for the persistent notion that men and women are unequal.

PAUL

The largest number of specific references to sexual relationship in the New Testament are to be found, of course, in the epistles of St Paul. In assessing their significance it is important to remember both their epistolary form and the eschatological framework of the apostle's thinking. Very often when St Paul makes a pronouncement he is answering a question which has been asked in a communication from one of the churches.[6] Because he was dealing with human situations, and not attempting a systematic exposition of the question under consideration, it is not surprising that he is sometimes inconsistent. The Apostle's

[6] *See* 1 Corinthians 7^{1a}.

critics have not always noticed that, with disarming humility, he sometimes says when dealing with marriage: 'I say this, as my own word, not as the Lord's' (1 Cor 7¹²). Not all modern prophets are careful to make this important distinction.

An examination of the seventh chapter of 1 Corinthians will illustrate the points just made. Some of the Christians at Corinth, influenced by the ultra-ascetical party, have enquired of St Paul whether they ought to give up sexual intercourse altogether. Now the Apostle, unlike Luther, Knox, and other later leaders of Christian thought was unmarried, and those who put the question may well have assumed that Paul would confirm their own ascetic tendencies. It is true that he does reveal his own personal preference for the single state. 'I should like you all to be as I am myself,' he says (verse 7). More than that, he cannot hide the fact that he has a certain dislike of the sex-relation. Indeed this whole chapter furnishes a fascinating study of the way in which sound practical advice about the place of coition in marriage is interspersed with such startling indications of personal prejudice as are contained in the assertion: 'It is a good thing for a man to have nothing to do with women' (verse 1*b*).

Of course, as we have said, such strong views as these must be set against the background of the Apostle's earnest, though mistaken, expectation of the imminent Return of the Lord. His whole outlook is coloured by this belief. 'It is my opinion, then, that in a time of stress like the present this is the best way for a man to live—it is best for a man to be as he is. . . . What I mean, my friends, is this. The time we live in will not last long. While it lasts, married men should be as if they had no wives. . . . For the whole frame of this world is passing away' (verses 26, 29, 31). When, however, full allowance has been made for Paul's urgent preoccupation with the Parousia, it is clear that he reveals a bias against marriage which is not wholly due to the utilitarian idea that, as the End is near, it is more sensible to concentrate on concerns other than matrimonial. To be sure, he nowhere goes to the lengths of the writer of the Book of Revelation who sees the host of the redeemed as 'men who did not defile themselves with women' (Rev 14[4]). St Paul directed that the women should keep silent in church, but refrained from suggesting that the music of heaven would be entirely provided by a male voice choir.

The Pauline teaching has often been misrepresented and misused. Some of the Church fathers, like Tertullian and Jerome, with whom we shall deal in the next chapter, appealed to the Apostle's authority but injected into his teaching ideas which were the product of their own warped thinking. Paul refused to identify chastity with celibacy as some would have wished him to do. Indeed one suspects that some of the more 'spiritual' brethren at Corinth must have been scandalized by aspects of the advice he gave. For Paul reveals a depth of understanding and a down-to-earth realism which are sadly lacking in the writings of many of the monkish theologians who later helped to tie the teaching of the Church in knots that are still far from completely unravelled. A few more quotations from the first Corinthian letter will suffice to establish the point: 'The husband must give the wife what is due to her, and the wife equally must give the husband his due. The wife cannot claim her body as her own; it is her husband's. Equally, the husband cannot claim his body as his own; it is his wife's. Do not deny yourselves to one another, except when you agree upon a temporary abstinence in order to devote yourselves to prayer; afterwards you may come together again; otherwise, for lack of self-control, you may be tempted by Satan' (7[3-5]). The modern Christian may feel that abstinence may hinder rather than help the prayers which he and his wife say together, but Paul is certainly not talking here as a rigid ascetic. To the unmarried Paul says: 'If they cannot control themselves, they should marry. Better be married than burn with vain desire' (7^9). We may regret the negative suggestion of marriage as a remedy against sin, which has been an element in the Christian tradition, but again there is a big difference between the permissive attitude of Paul and the entirely negative and often scurrilous attitude to marriage which we shall meet in the next chapter. There is a note of human concern and understanding in the words: 'If, however, you do marry, there is nothing wrong in it; and if a virgin marries, she has done no wrong. But those who marry will have pain and grief in this bodily life, and my aim is to spare you' (7^{28}).

A more detailed examination of other sections of Paul's teaching would not take us much farther. If his thought about the relationship of men and women is examined with care it yields much that is of undying value. But to plead now for a careful and sympathetic interpretation of the Pauline teaching about sex is rather like locking the stable door after the horse has bolted. For, indeed, that horse, in the form of a spreading heresy, has gone galloping down the centuries treading many fine truths in the mire of human misery. To change the metaphor, there is a cloud which hangs over the Apostle's thinking on this all-important subject. It may be no bigger than a man's hand, but it is there. It will later spread across the sky and cast a grey shadow over the relationships of men and women for whom the experience of salvation could not permeate their sex-life, because there, in the inner citadel of human being, the lamp of truth burned with a glow too feeble to dispel the darkness of error and sin. That cloud is the dualistic heresy, the history of which we have begun to trace—the idea that there are two creations, not one, and that matter and spirit must for ever be at war with each other.

We turn now once again to the second aspect of our subject which demands special attention, and which is so obviously related to the first. What did Paul believe and teach about the relative status of men and women?

There is no doubt at all about the fact that women held a position in the fellowship of the early Church which was quite exceptional by the standards of the age. It is interesting, though not always easy, to piece together the references in the New Testament which show that women fulfilled regular ministries with specific functions. St Paul refers to the fact that women prophesied in the church at Corinth.[7] In his letter to the Romans, the Apostle says: 'I commend to you Phoebe, a fellow-Christian who holds office in the congregation at Cenchreae' (16¹). The opening salutation in the letter to Philemon refers to 'Apphia our sister' who is a leader in 'the congregation at your house'. The first letter to Timothy contains an interesting passage which indicates that some widows were incorporated into an order and undertook special duties in the service of the church. That the arrangement was not without its difficulties is made plain by the instructions concerning women under the age of sixty. 'Younger widows may not be placed on the roll. For when their passions draw them away from Christ, they hanker after marriage and stand condemned for breaking their troth with him. Moreover, in going round from house to house they learn to be idle, and worse than idle, gossips and busybodies, speaking of things better left unspoken. It is my wish, therefore, that young widows shall marry again, have children, and preside over a home; then they will give no opponent occasion

[7] 1 Corinthians 11⁴.

for slander. For there have in fact been widows who have taken the wrong turning and gone to the devil' (5^{11-15}). Assuming the Pauline authorship of this letter, it is a little amusing to find the Apostle here apparently only too anxious to get the young widows married off as the best solution of a problem which had damaged the life of the Church.

In spite of the position held by women in the Church of the New Testament, the Apostolic teaching, as might be expected, accepts the headship of the male as the divinely appointed basis of sexual order. The attempt is made to give a firm theological foundation to this conception by linking it directly with the Genesis story of creation. The Apostle's words to Timothy are an example of what male theologians can do with the Scriptures when they employ them uncritically; 'I do not permit a woman to be a teacher, nor must woman domineer over man; she should be quiet. For Adam was created first, and Eve afterwards; and it was not Adam who was deceived; it was the woman who, yielding to deception, fell into sin. Yet she will be saved through motherhood' (1 Tim 2^{12-15}). This might surely be described as a strange scriptural sequence of *non sequiturs*. The same point is even more specifically stated in the First Epistle to the Corinthians. 'But I wish you to understand that, while every man has Christ for his Head, woman's head is man, as Christ's Head is God' (11^3). This passage precedes the directions about women covering their heads in church. But at the end Paul flings in the paradoxical comment: 'And yet, in Christ's fellowship woman is as essential to man as man to woman. If woman was made out of man, it is through woman that man now comes to be; and God is the source of all' (11^{11-12}).

Considerable confusion has been caused by the apparent inconsistency of St Paul with regard to whether or not women should prophesy in church. As we have seen in the First Epistle to the Corinthians he assumes that women do prophesy; he also gives directions about the covering of their heads. But later on he seems to forbid them to speak at all. 'As in all congregations of God's people, women should not address the meeting. They have no licence to speak, but should keep their place as the law directs. If there is something they want to know, they can ask their own husbands at home. It is a shocking thing that a woman should address the congregation' (14^{34-5}). It is true that there is some doubt as to whether these words are authentic, but, assuming that they are, we may conjecture that they refer to some specific reference by Paul's Corinthian correspondents to the fact that some of the women had been opening their mouths too much. They probably had caused disorder by interrupting the preacher to ask the meaning of what he was saying. The incompleteness of the glimpses we get of the situation in the early Church encourages speculation. If something of the kind suggested is not the explanation of the passage just quoted the only alternative is that Paul is not consistent on the point about female participation in Church services. It certainly appears from the First Epistle to Timothy quoted earlier that later in his life Paul's views hardened on this question. Those who reject the Pauline authorship of that Epistle will take the passage as evidence of the wish in the first post-apostolic age to curtail the freedom of expression of women in the Church.

One more passage must be referred to, and that is the resounding declaration of the principle of spiritual oneness in the Epistle to the Galations: 'There is no such thing as Jew and Greek, slave and freeman, male and female; for you are all one person in Christ Jesus'(3^{28}). It would be easy enough to charge the great Apostle with inconsistency when setting this verse alongside some of the other things he said. The really important point to note, however, is that he here enunciates a principle which was of even greater significance than he could see or understand. It is a seminal idea which is to grow in the minds of men and women, and indeed today we are only beginning to realize the far-reaching implications of it. If, in the intervening centuries, men preferred to remember the less egalitarian pronouncements of the Apostle and buried his great principle instead of allowing it to leaven their thought and life, he is not to be blamed. Perhaps the worst thing of all is that the Galatian enunciation of the one-ness of male and female in Christ has been accepted as a statement of 'the spiritual equality of men and women', but, because of a disastrous divorce between spiritual and material, has not challenged those basic inequalities which have impoverished the lives of women, and of men, and robbed society of the rich rewards of true partnership.

In the next chapter we glance at those intervening centuries and recall the names of some of those who helped to transmit the Christian teaching and mould the tradition regarding the man-woman relationship.

CHAPTER TWO

VARIATIONS ON A THEME

THE ERRONEOUS belief that physical sexuality is tainted or evil, and the false notion that man is fundamentally superior to woman have acted as blinkers, limiting vision and hindering progress. Both these ideas are woven into the fabric of Christian traditional teaching as it has come down to us. Of course, the tradition has been subject to change, and some Christian thinkers have seen farther than others. But during the first five centuries of the Church—the 'five hundred long years', as Dr James Moffat has called them—our fathers in the faith laid down certain basic presuppositions which remained virtually unchallenged for a thousand years. Marriage is described as a 'sad tragedy' and a 'galling burden'. Since the minister of the Word and sacraments must be holy he must remain celibate and free of the contamination of the fleshly entanglements of marriage. Such an attitude is inevitably linked with a jaundiced view of woman. Tertullian refers to her as 'the devil's gateway'. No wonder the saying grew up that 'there are three sexes—men, women, and priests'.

Although there will be widespread agreement with the contention of this lecture that it is urgently necessary to correct the false teaching of the past, justice requires that we look sympathetically at the reasons for the persistence of those errors. Some of the Church fathers spoke scurrilously about sex and marriage, but as one reads the story of their fierce struggle with passions that were a problem rather than a prize, indignation often gives place to pity, and sometimes, if one is honest, to a feeling of sympathy.

Here were men battling with the temptations which we have to face. Who among us feels justified in casting the first stone?

THE EARLY CHRISTIAN HERESIES

Before we proceed, then, to a necessarily critical review of the teaching of some of those who helped to mould the Christian tradition, we pause to remind ourselves of three important facts. The first is that, as we saw in the last chapter, from the beginning Christianity was subject to the pressures and influences of alien religions and philosophies. 'It used to be the fashion . . . to say that Christianity appeared at the psychological moment when religion had died out of the world and atheism had left a void waiting to be filled. We know now on the contrary that there had been a striking revival of religious interest. The Church did not step forth on to an empty stage, but into an arena full of warring sects and rival faiths.'[1]

In these days we hear little about heresy, and only rarely is a minister of the Church arraigned on a charge of preaching false doctrine. This, of course, may be partly the result of a certain religious apathy, but it is mainly due to the fact that in the early centuries of the Christian era the Church fought against powerful enemies that threatened the doctrinal foundations on which its faith is built, and overcame them.

It is significant that one of the earliest forms of heretical thought was that of Docetism (from the Greek verb '*dokein*', 'to seem'). The Docetics accepted the divinity of Christ but taught that His bodily appearance was a phantasy. The insistence in the Johannine writings on the reality of the incarnation of the Son of God is a deliberate rebuttal of this false teaching. Docetism is an illustration of one of the basic elements in all Christian

[1] *A History of the Early Church*, J. W. C. Wand (Methuen, 2nd ed., 1945).

heresy: the inability or unwillingness of men to hold together what God has joined. The early Christian apologists, like Quadratus, Aristides and Justin Martyr were concerned with various aspects of the challenge to the fundamental beliefs which characterized the uniqueness of the Christian religion.

The greatest enemy within the world of ideas with which the Christian Church had to contend from the beginning was Gnosticism (from the Greek word '*gnosis*', 'knowledge'). The influence of this system of beliefs is to be seen in many of the heretical movements which bedevilled the life of the infant Church. There were three main types of Gnosticism. The first is associated with the teaching of Simon Magus in Syria; the second emanated from Alexandria, and the greatest of its exponents was the poet Valentinus; the third was of a rather different kind and its chief adherent was Marcion, whom Polycarp described as the 'first-born of Satan'. A detailed description of the differing forms of Gnosticism is beyond our present purpose; the important point to stress is that the central emphasis was upon the essential dualism of God and the world, of soul and matter. This is the idea that in one form or another has dominated the old religions of the East.

Gnosticism ceased to exist in an organized form. It was defeated by a Church which held in its hand the Hebrew bible, and in its heart the strong commanding evidence that God had visited His people, 'widest extremes to join'. But the victory was not by any means complete, and the extent to which the ideas of Gnosticism affected the outlook of the Christian Church is apparent again and again as we listen to the teachings and confessions of our fathers in the faith, especially when they are speaking of sexual matters.

THE IDEA OF RENUNCIATION

The second important fact to be born in mind in studying the testimony of Christian writers is that 'In every human heart, except, possibly, the utterly depraved, we find a yearning for self-surrender rising at times to a passion. . . . This imperial note of our higher natures can never wholly be silenced by the lower, and finds expression in every form of religion, however degraded or unreasoning. For the Christian at least, self-surrender is the imperative call of the Master.'[2]

For almost a thousand years this desire for renunciation found expression in the monastic movement. The word 'monastic' derives from the Greek '*monos*', 'alone', and is used to denote those who live apart from the world, either as individuals or in communities. The origin of this way of life is not, of course, wholly Christian, for there were monks in Egypt, and there were the ascetics of the Orphic Societies, before the rise of Christian monasticism. There were also the Jewish sects known as the Essenes and the Therapeutae who followed the same calling.

Christian monasticism began in Alexandria and from the beginning was closely associated with those ascetic practices which sought by mortifying the flesh to gain deliverance for the soul. The influence of Gnosticism was very much greater in the East than in the West—mainly because St Augustine turned his back on Manichaeism, which was really a restatement of Gnostic ideas. But in the East it was a most powerful factor in moulding the monastic tradition. Symeon Stylites is probably the best-known of the Eastern recluses. He was born (*c.* A.D. 390) at Sis near Nicopolis and lived the last thirty-seven years of his life on the top of a pillar. It is not surprising that Theodoret described him as 'that great miracle of the

[2] *The Evolution of the Monastic Ideal*, H. B. Workman (Epworth, 1927), p. 3.

world'. Even before moving into this most undesirable residence he had pursued a life of most rigorous asceticism. He lived in a cave with his right leg fastened to an iron chain. When the circle of leather which protected his leg from the chain was removed it contained twenty fat bugs. His admirers evidently thought this fact worth recording, and later, when he moved to the top of the pillar, they cherished the worms that fell from his body. Havelock Ellis must have had this sort of thing in mind when he said: 'The Church killed the bath.'

Many endeavoured to emulate this peculiar form of piety. There are records of saints living in tubs suspended from poles. One occupied a cistern and existed on five figs a day. Others lived like animals in the deserts, eating grass. One hermit called Acepsurias became so bent and hairy that one day a shepherd shot him, mistaking him for a goat. Another named Macarius was one day stung by a gnat. He not unnaturally killed the insect, but then, overcome with remorse at having failed to bear the mortification with resignation, he went to live for six months in some marshes which were notorious for the size of their gnats and the virulence of their attack. It is at this point that the exploits of the saints begin to read like a horror comic.

Although in the West there were some examples of excesses not dissimilar from the kind just described, on the whole the developments within Western monasticism were along much saner and more practical lines. The towering figures of St Gregory and St Bernard symbolize a different ideal. This is reflected in the words of St Basil: 'If fasting hinders you from labour, it is better to eat, remembering that you are athletes, workmen of Jesus Christ.'

Whether, however, we are considering the fantastic austerities of the Eastern hermits, or the more appealing

VARIATIONS ON A THEME

witness of the Western monastic orders, the point to remember is that, though the ways of expressing it are often strangely misguided and even morbid, we are witnessing the desire of man for self-surrender which is present in every form of religion.

THE PROTEST AGAINST DECADENCE
The third fact which deserves mention is that the ascetic way of life was in part a protest against the sensuality, luxury and moral disorder of a rotten society. The idea of renunciation was given positive content in the three-fold vow of poverty, chastity, and obedience, and of these three undoubtedly the second was regarded as the most important. The exaltation of virginity which is so common a theme in Christian literature, at any rate from Tertullian onwards, resulted in the most absurd relations between men and women. A monk called Prior refused for fifty years to see any member of his family. His bishop was approached by the monk's sister with a request for an interview with her brother. This was granted but the monk took good care to keep his eyes shut tight all the time they were conversing together. Another monk who saw an abbess coming towards him turned out of the path, but not soon enough to escape hearing her caustic but sincere rebuke: 'If you were a true monk you would not know whether we were women or not.' One of the most revolting of all the stories is that of a young girl of Alexandria who, when she discovered that it was the brightness of her eyes which had caused a young man to try to make love to her, took up a weaver's shuttle and dug them out.

It is, indeed, difficult to convince most modern readers that there is anything at all to commend in behaviour of this sort. They equate it with the action of those who, when Sir Walter Scott as a child said he liked his soup, poured half a pint of cold water into it. A more healthy-minded generation, confronted with the record, turns from it either with disgust or with plain incredulity. Perhaps, however, a closer acquaintance with the depravities of a corrupt world, and a deeper sympathy with the passionate quest for holiness, might mitigate a little the harsh condemnation which falls rather too easily from our lips. Some words of Dean Inge are worth recalling: 'When all is said that can or ought to be said against the strangest aberration in all human history, there are profound truths in the ascetic ideal, which modern civilization is neglecting at its great peril. In the first place, a cheap Gospel is doomed to ineffectiveness; religion demands real sacrifices of pleasure and comfort. And it is good that there should be specialists in this as in every other pursuit. There is such a thing as a vocation to the saintly life. The renunciations which we sometimes suppose to have been made from a perverse love of being miserable were mostly made in order to concentrate the mind and will on the one supreme quest.'[3] We will bear this caveat in mind as we glance now at the names of some of the most important Christian thinkers of the past.

TERTULLIAN

Tertullian was one of the very influential ancient Christian writers. He taught that though, of course, marriage is good, virginity is better. Like many another writer he damns marriage with faint praise. The parable of the sower is misapplied to suggest that the wedded state produces thirty-fold compared with the sixty-fold of widowhood or the hundred-fold of virginity. In a dissertation *Ad Uxorem* Tertullian speaks of the 'most bitter pleasure of children', and seems to interpret literally the word of

[3] *Christian Ethics and Modern Problems* (Hodder & Stoughton, 1930).

Jesus about 'hating' father and mother, spouse and child. His own true feelings and inner tensions are revealed in his assurance to his own wife, that their sexual acts within marriage will be left behind in heaven because God regards such things as frivolous and impure. His references to his sexual misdemeanours reveal an exaggerated sense of guilt. He is very obviously trying to run away from his own sexuality and every time he looks over his shoulder he finds it is catching him up. His views on women are summed up in the phrase already quoted in the opening paragraph of this chapter.

JEROME

Jerome is even more extravagant in his praise of virginity. He is always condemning in others in excessively violent language the sins of which he himself was guilty in his younger days. He is a perfect text-book example of the man who is at war with himself. He tries to subdue his unruly passions and to mortify the flesh, but even in the midst of his ascetic exercises he is tormented by visions of feminine beauty and cannot escape the seduction of their charm. The best he can find to say about marriage is that it produces virgins: 'I praise marriage and wedlock, but only because they beget celibates. I gather roses from thorns, gold from the earth, pearls from shells.' He castigates Woman because it was she who caused Adam to be ejected from Paradise.

There is something offensive about the way in which both Tertullian and Jerome seem to cast around for the most abusive words they can find when speaking of the relationship in which so many have found blessing beyond the power of the finest language to describe. However much sympathy we may feel for them as men who failed to come to terms with their own natures, it is to be regretted that they exercised a considerable influence on Christian thought.

AUGUSTINE

We pass now to Augustine whose importance was in every way greater than that of Tertullian and Jerome. He exercised a determinative influence on the development of Christian thought, second only to that of the Apostle Paul himself. Again, his teaching provides us with a fascinating illustration of the truth that men's beliefs are enormously affected by their experience. The story of his youthful adventures and of his restless quest for truth is well-known. He was for a time deeply influenced by the Manichees whose dualistic doctrine associated the body with evil, and bade men seek salvation by means of ascetic practices and escape from the imprisonment of the flesh. In the Sixth Book of his *Confessions* he says: 'While I thus desired a happy life, I yet feared to seek it in its true abode, and I fled from it while yet I sought it. For I thought I should be too miserable if I were deprived of the embraces of a woman; and I considered not the medicine and the power of Thy mercy in the cure of that infirmity for thereof I had taken no experience. . . . Thus I, fast bound with the diseases of the flesh and with the deadly sweetness thereof, dragged my fetters after me, fearing lest they should be loosed.'[4]

How hard Augustine tried to escape from this dualistic emphasis and from the memories of earlier sexual experiences which rose up like half-welcome ghosts to condemn him. 'Very toys of toys and vanities of vanities they were, those ancient favourites of mine which detained me; they caught at the fleshy garment of my soul and softly whispered, "Dost thou cast us off?" and "Can it be that henceforth we shall not be with thee for ever?" But those things which they suggested by their "this or that", what was it they suggested, O my God? Oh may Thy mercy guard

[4] *The Confessions of St Augustine*, translated by Sir Tobie Matthew, p. 157.

the soul of me Thy servant, from all the filthiness and shame they meant! I heard them indeed, though now less than half their former size, not daring to withstand me to my face; but softly muttering behind my back, and plucking slyly at me as I went from them, as if in hope of making me look round.... But by this time it spoke even this but very faintly. For in that quarter to which the face of my soul was turned, and whither I yet nimbled to advance, the chaste dignity of continence discovered herself. Cheerful she was, not dissolutely enticing, but sweetly inducing me to advance and to fear nothing; yea, stretching forth to receive and to embrace me those dear hands of hers, that were full of good examples. Many there were both young men and maidens, yea and of all ages, grave widows and aged virgins, and continence herself in every one of them, not barren but a fruitful mother of children, of joys begotten by Thee, O Lord, her husband. And she smiled upon me with a mirthful encouragement, as if she said, "canst thou not do what all of these have done?" '[5]

These quotations are more revealing than any extended commentary on the thought and outlook of Augustine. It is interesting to notice how the very description of continence herself (note the feminine pronoun) is couched in the language which lovers use. He had become dissatisfied with the Manichees, and associated himself briefly with the Skeptics, before he found an answer to his intellectual quest for truth in the writings of Plotinus. But the turmoil of his emotions was only brought to an end by conversion to the Christian faith. This occurred when, bidden by some inner voice, he took up the Bible and read: 'Let us behave with decency as befits the day: no revelling or drunkenness, no debauchery or vice, no quarrels or jealousies! Let Christ Jesus himself be the

[5] Ibid. Book VIII, pp. 214-15.

armour that you wear; give no more thought to satisfying the bodily appetites' (Rom 13¹³⁻¹⁴). He records that 'instantly with the end of this sentence, as by a clear and constant light infused into my heart, the darkness of all former doubts was driven away'.[6] Later he adds: 'For Thou didst so convert me to Thyself, as that I do no more desire a wife nor any other ambition of this world.'[7]

Thus was Monica's wayward son converted. History has much more to tell us about Augustine, but nothing more about either the girl to whom he was engaged but never married, or the mistress who bore him a son but was sent back to her home in Africa vowing that 'she would never know man more'. But history is largely a male story and those who now are interested in 'the woman's angle' must fill in the gaps with their own speculations. For the Bishop of Hippo, Woman was branded with the reproach that it was she who led Man into sin.

Augustine's sexual experience colours his theological outlook and his interpretation of the Genesis story. This, of course, is quite inevitable, for there is no such thing as an entirely objective theologian. In the case of Augustine, however, the connection between his own experiences as recorded in the *Confessions*, and his theology, is crystal clear—and, we may add, in many ways regrettable.

Augustine was compelled by the teaching of the Bible to regard sex and marriage as good since God had created and ordained them. But he believed very strongly that sex had been specially infected by sin. The shame of Adam and Eve which caused them to cover their genitals is the result of a new and deadly impulse called concupiscence. This affects the whole of life but is particularly active in the sexual realm. The argument is put forward

[6] *The Confessions of St Augustine*, VIII. 217.   [7] Ibid. p. 218.

that one of the results of concupiscence is that Adam and Eve no longer have control over their sexual organs. Just as the man and woman are disobedient to God so their own members are disobedient to their masters. Ideally coition should be without heat or passion, and in paradise the congress of the sexes would be calm and devoid of those animal excitements which Augustine finds so repellent. Here is a strange confusion of thought. Of course it is true that sin often displays itself in lack of self-control, but when Augustine suggested that God's intention was that procreation should be secured by the mechanical obedience of the organs of reproduction acting in accordance with the dictates of the human will, he was, of course, showing an understandable but unfortunate ignorance of the biological processes which God Himself designed.

The reader may wonder how Augustine could hold these views and still accept marriage as a good estate ordained by God. He did so by employing a somewhat tortuous argument. Marriage, in his view, does not alter the fact that coition, even when performed for the express purpose of procreation, is tainted with concupiscence, but such coition is excused of its sinfulness. It is, however, the means whereby sin is transmitted to the next generation. But what if the motive is pleasure or the relief of incontinence? No doubt Augustine would have liked to condemn outright any intercourse which did not specifically aim at procreation. But he could not very well do so when St Paul plainly allows it (1 Cor 7[5]). He says, therefore, that such embraces are sinful, but the sin is such as will be pardoned, and to be distinguished from the unmitigated evil of fornication or adultery. This unsatisfactory conclusion is the result of trying to make the best of a bad job.

The further Augustine goes the worse it gets. He makes suggestions which are nowhere to be found in the writings of St Paul. He seizes upon the Virgin Birth of our Saviour as evidence of the essentially sinful nature of coition. Paul believed that sin is passed on from one generation to the next, through the flesh, but he did not imply that the evil of coition is responsible for that transmission. Augustine believed that the reason for the Virgin Birth of Jesus was that if He had been born as the result of normal intercourse He would have been tainted by that very fact. Incidentally it is interesting that the later dogma of the immaculate conception of the Virgin Mary should have been invented, with, presumably, the same erroneous idea in mind. The next step should surely be an attempt to explain away the brothers of Jesus.[8] This would require great ingenuity, unless someone could dig up an ancient manuscript which proved that Joseph died shortly after leaving the stable at Bethlehem.

It is all of a piece with Augustine's teaching that he should make the suggestion that Christians would be well advised to leave the production of candidates for salvation to the pagans. They can get the children born and the Christians can get them born again. The conclusion that we had better leave our dirty work to the unbelievers is rendered scarcely less palatable by the obvious sincerity with which the suggestion is made. It is also, perhaps, not irrelevant to reflect that it seems to imply a rather too facile view of the evangelistic mission of the Church. Would to God that the task of converting the heathen were as easy as Augustine would here seem to be implying. He appears to take no account of the fact that the most fruitful field of recruitment for the Kingdom of God is always the home where children are brought up in the nurture and admonition of the Lord.

We have given considerable space to Augustine because of his importance in the development of the Christian

[8] *See* Luke 8:19-20.

tradition. If his approach to the problems of human sexuality is on the whole distasteful to us, and if sometimes it rouses our indignation, we may perhaps allow ourselves one last glimpse of him. In Book X of the *Confessions* he admits that, though in his waking hours he is free from the compelling temptations which once brought him low, by night he is often troubled by lustful dreams. And, in fact, the dreams are so vivid as to be very nearly like the real thing. One is reminded of the question put by the schoolboy: 'Do you believe in sex before marriage?' The real reply to that, of course, is that sex is not something you are free to believe or disbelieve. It is something you must live with from the moment of birth, or rather of conception, to the moment of death. If you fly from it up some avenue of escape you will meet it coming down the other way. This was something Augustine proved but did not realize. And with him, while the apocalyptic belief of St Paul has ceased to be of great significance, the canker of dualism has eaten into the fabric of his mind.

A NOTE ON SPIRITUAL MARRIAGES
AND SINGLE WOMEN

The Western attempt at the beginning of the fourth century to impose a rule of abstinence from coition on all bishops, presbyters, and deacons was only partially successful. The natural instincts and passions of men inevitably proved stronger than a rule which is only worthy of obedience if it is founded on right reason and true understanding of God's purposes.

One extraordinary manifestation of sexual asceticism was syneisaktism, or spiritual marriage. Under this system men and women lived together in close intimacy and complete continence. It requires little knowledge or imagination to picture the excessive strains imposed upon many of those who entered upon such a relationship.

Although the phrase is sometimes used there is really, of course, no such thing as 'a purely spiritual relationship' between human beings. Any attempt to deny this fundamental fact of life is fraught with perils. Stern efforts were made to suppress an experiment which had inevitably resulted in a great deal of scandal.

Although the world of the Church historian is very much a man's world, a thin line of women stretches back across the centuries consisting of individuals with special gifts who were esteemed and employed in the services of the Church. Gorgonia, and the sister of Gregory of Nyssa are examples. In most cases these women were honoured because of their vows of continence and their service was always regarded as subordinate to that of men. None of these women, however, played any significant part in the formulation of the Christian tradition regarding sex and marriage, though, of course, it goes without saying that without women there would be no sexual tradition!

THOMAS AQUINAS

After Augustine came the period of what Professor Latourette in his panoramic account of the rise and spread of Christianity calls 'The Great Recession'. 'For more than four centuries . . . in the numbers of those who called themselves Christian, in apparent inner vitality as expressed in fresh movements inspired by the faith, in the moral and spiritual qualities of the churches which were the official vehicles of the Gospel, and in its prominence in the total human scene, Christianity lost ground.'[9] But following this dark period when the Roman Empire and the Graeco-Roman Culture were in the process of accelerating disintegration there came a time of resurgence and advance. The most remarkable period came in the

[9] *A History of Christianity* (Eyre & Spottiswoode), pp. 269-70.

thirteenth century. This was the age of Dante and of St Francis, of Innocent the Third, who carried the papacy to its highest point in history, and of Thomas Aquinas, the greatest of the medieval theologians. The system of Aquinas was sanctioned by papal decree as the theology of the Roman Catholic Church, and he is, therefore, important in this brief review of the great formative influences in the development of the thought of the Church on sexual relationship.

Aquinas, like Augustine and St Paul, was unmarried. Unlike the Bishop of Hippo, his life was comparatively uneventful. He devoted himself to study, to teaching and to writing. His brief life was one of intense mental activity. In his *Summa Theologica* he achieved a remarkable synthesis of the thought of those two intellectual giants, Aristotle and Augustine.

The Thomist interpretation of sex begins, like that of Augustine, with the biblical account of creation. There at the beginning it is clear that the position of woman is subordinate to that of man. Eve is to be Adam's 'helpmeet', and this is interpreted as meaning that she was created to serve in a subordinate role. Aquinas reiterated without questioning them such Aristotelian assertions as that man is essentially more reasonable than woman, and of superior intellectual capacity. He does, however, reveal a real measure of humane consideration in insisting that a man must treat his wife as a person and not as an object to gratify his desires.

The stress on the use of reason and the life of the mind predisposed Aquinas, as it had done Augustine before him, to view with suspicion the powerful physical forces connected with the sex instinct which disrupt the life of serene mental contemplation. He does not deny that sex is God-given but is in agreement with Augustine in believing that it has been altogether corrupted by concupiscence. It is cheering, though, to find him taking a more positive view of pleasure, which is by no means always evil.

There is, however, in the writings of Aquinas the same wearisome insistence on the superiority of the virgin state over that of marriage. He believes this view to be amply confirmed by the example of Jesus who chose a virgin as His mother and Himself remained virgin, and by the teaching of St Paul who obviously preferred the single state. Marriage is a remedy for sin and a means of stemming the wild course of lustful desire.

Catholic dogma was carefully and fully defined by the Council of Trent. Marriage is a sacrament, and divorce is impossible. Within marriage coition is only right when the motive is either procreation or the satisfying of natural desire that would otherwise lead to lust. The desire for pleasure is condemned.

LUTHER AND CALVIN

There is a measure of relief in turning to the teaching of the great Reformers. Not only were Luther and Calvin married men, but there is a robust and positive element in their approach to sex and marriage which marks a real advance in experience and understanding.

Viewed from our own vantage-point in time, Luther, the chief pioneer of Protestantism, may well appear as an odd mixture of unexpected liberalism and unresolved tensions, with more than a dash of plain vulgarity. His detractors have certainly made the most of his more earthy sayings, but, like the rest of our fathers in the faith, he must be viewed in the context of his own day.

Luther rejected outright the idea of the superiority of virginity over marriage and repudiated the rule of clerical celibacy. This break with tradition was, in the realm of sexual relationship, the greatest of the contributions of the Reformers. Not only was it a most important movement away from an entrenched error, but it helped to liberate later generations from the domination of monkish theologians with no experience of marriage to inform their judgements.

Luther goes out of his way to advocate marriage. He is so impressed with the force and power of the sexual urge that he believes celibacy can only be regarded as a vocation for the very few. To a friend to whom he writes on the subject he counsels marriage with the least possible delay: 'Your body demands it; God wills and insists upon it.' His earthy realism sometimes scandalized the decorous, as when he gave the famous advice: 'If the wife refuse, let the maid come.'

His main reasons for insisting on the duty of all but a few to marry are that God has ordained it, and that no one is free from the compulsions of lust. It is obvious from this that it would be quite wrong to suppose that from the time of the Reformation onwards there were two quite different and opposed sexual traditions labelled 'Catholic' and 'Protestant'. In fact many of the beliefs which were held by Augustine and Aquinas are re-echoed in the teaching of Luther. He returns repeatedly to the theme of the all-pervasiveness of sin. The results of sin on sex are seen in the ravages of lust, the pains of childbirth, the subjugation of woman, and the sense of shame connected with nakedness and sexuality. He believes that coition and communion with God are mutually exclusive. Marriage is a hospital for the sick, and sex is, when all is said and done, a regrettable necessity. The sin of sex in marriage, however, is something God winks at because wedlock prevents many much worse evils.

It will be noted that Luther's realism is almost wholly concerned with the sexual needs of man. The idea that woman has parallel needs has yet to dawn with any real degree of understanding on the masterful males preoccupied with their own passions. In one respect the reformed attitude to the family, whilst it emphasized the privilege and responsibility of parenthood, militated against the possibility of an enhanced status for women. The new emphasis on the authority of the Scriptures resulted in an underlining of the patriarchal authority exemplified in Hebrew Society as the model on which Christian family life should be built.

Another influence which robbed the Reformation of some of its liberating power in the sexual realm was a certain prudishness which tended to encourage a disproportionate severity in the Protestant outlook on sexual misdemeanours.

Calvin's teaching is very similar to that of Luther. He, too, thought celibacy an almost impossible ideal for the majority, and indeed he pungently observes that it would be difficult to find one convent in ten that was not a brothel. In marriage, which is a remedy against sin, husband and wife must consider each other's sexual needs, but they must be careful not to fall into the evil of excessive pleasure in their carnal relationship. Calvin certainly displays an unusual degree of sympathetic understanding of women and their needs, and on the whole he is less pessimistic about sex than Luther.

Before bringing this chapter to a close it will be as well to emphasize again the point which is made at the beginning. It is essential when studying the life and thought of those who have helped to mould the Christian tradition to try always to see them against the background of their own times. It is easy enough to condemn what may seem to us to be inexcusable excesses or absurd distortions of the truth. But it is far more important to understand than to condemn. It must be remembered, too, that in this chapter we have concentrated on one aspect of the teaching of our fathers. No attempt has been made to judge the value of their contribution to other and wider fields of thought. There is, too, the fact which ought by now to be clear enough, that in adumbrating beliefs which are, in some cases, no longer acceptable to us, they were not guilty of taking a doctrine of original purity and polluting it by the perversity of their own warped thinking. The facts are very much more complicated than that. They inherited a complex system of ideas to which many differing cultures had contributed. The waters of truth must perforce flow along channels dug by men, and this means that inevitably they get contaminated by the mud of human sin and misunderstanding. Not one of us can claim to possess a filter which is able to restore the stream to its pristine transparency. There is laid upon us the duty of seeking always the mind of Him who is the Truth.

Following the work of the Reformers there was a long period during which little significant progress was made in the Christian study of the relationship of men and women. In more recent times, however, a number of factors have combined to undermine some of the emphases in the Christian interpretation of sex. We must now turn to these elements in an erosion which has already had far-reaching results.

CHAPTER THREE

A TRUMPET VOICE SOUNDS

IT IS ONE of the ironies of history that when in 1930 Stanley Baldwin unveiled the statue to Emmeline Pankhurst in the Victoria Tower Gardens in London the music for the occasion was provided by a police band. So the men whose duties had more than once required them to arrest this turbulent leader of the suffragettes were present to honour her memory. Moreover, as if to emphasize the inescapable point that a revolution had taken place, the musicians of the police force were conducted by Dame Ethel Smyth, the composer, colourfully attired in the grey and scarlet robes of a doctor of music.

In delivering the Eleanor Rathbone Memorial Lecture in 1960 Lord Denning said: 'She [Eleanor Rathbone] in her lifetime [1870-1946] witnessed one of the greatest revolutions of all time, and she played a significant part in it. I refer to the emancipation of women. At her birth women were in subjection to men. At her death they had achieved for the most part equality with men. Their legal status is now equal to that of men. Their economic status is approaching equality.'[1]

Few would disagree with Lord Denning's judgement; the only qualification which need be added is the reminder that there are many parts of the world where women are still shackled by the chains of subordinate status. Of course, their time will come, for the trumpet voice which calls to freedom echoes round the earth, and all over the world the winds of change are blowing through windows shattered by the hammer-blows of

[1] *The Equality of Women* (London, 1960), p. 1.

women intent upon emancipation. In this chapter our remarks will be mainly confined to the women's movement in Britain.

THE GROWTH OF DEMOCRACY

In England, as G. M. Trevelyan reminds us, 'The demand for the political enfranchisement of women was the outcome of a very considerable degree of social enfranchisement already accomplished'.[2] The latter half of the long reign of Queen Victoria saw the development of democratic tendencies which were to gather momentum in the twentieth century, sweeping away old landmarks and altering the pattern of society in a variety of ways. The Reform Bill of 1867 gave the vote to the working men of the towns; three years later Parliament provided for universal primary education; competitive examination became the accepted method of entry to the Civil Service; the power of the Trade Unions was steadily growing; and, not least, the professional and social emancipation of women developed along the lines advocated in John Stuart Mill's *Subjection of Women*. This book, published in 1869, provided much useful ammunition for the feminists in this and other countries.

THE EFFECT OF INDUSTRIALIZATION

The real foundations for woman's rapid rise, however, were laid during the period of the Industrial Revolution. Towards the end of the eighteenth century a great deal of misery and unemployment for single women was caused by the rapid decay of the cottage industries which proliferated up and down the land. This decay was caused by the advent of the new machines which did more quickly and efficiently work that had formerly been done by hand. Many women, thus deprived of their livelihood,

[2] *English Social History* (Longmans, 1944), p. 552.

went to work for big capitalist farmers. Such field work, which had always been occasional among women in rural areas, now became for many an all-round-the-year occupation. Later more and more women found employment in factories. There the wages were scandalously low and it was the pressure of sheer need which drove many girls to a life of prostitution. However, when conditions improved, factory work not only brought to women a real measure of economic independence, but it also resulted in removing from working-class homes the dirt and smell of some of those cottage industries which had made them very unpleasant places.

TRADE UNIONISM

One of the most fascinating chapters in the annals of Trade Unionism is the story of the strike of the match girls in Bryant & May's factory in the East End of London in 1888. Interestingly enough this really began with a meeting of the Fabian Society in a quiet house in Bloomsbury. One summer evening certain members of that Society listened to a paper on 'Female Labour' read by Miss Clementina Black, the first woman ever to be appointed as a factory inspector. The paper referred to the fact that the London match girls were paid twopence-farthing a gross for the matchboxes they made. The strips of wood, coloured paper, labels and sandpaper were provided by the firm; but they had to find their own paste and string. During the discussion which followed, one of those present, H. H. Champion, struck a match with a flourish and moved a resolution calling on the members of the meeting to boycott Messrs Bryant & May by declining to buy or use their matches. What was more to the point, he suggested that Annie Besant should publicize the scandal in the *Link*—a paper which she ran with the help of W. T. Stead, the Christian Editor of the *Pall Mall Gazette*.

Annie Besant was a most remarkable woman. She had contracted an entirely unsuitable marriage with an Anglican clergyman. She had a brilliant and inquiring mind and found herself tortured with doubts about the orthodox beliefs of the Church. It is a pity that when she went for advice to Dr Pusey at Oxford that great scholar could find nothing more helpful to say to her than: 'It is not your duty to ascertain the Truth: it is your duty to accept and believe the Truth as laid down by the Church.' This was the last straw. Annie Besant left her husband and set out on that astonishing career during which she became notorious as the Vice-President of the National Secular Society. She was a compelling speaker. She was involved with Bradlaugh in the famous litigation over the Knowlton pamphlet which advocated birth control. There was a religious fervour about everything she did, and she was converted to Theosophy in 1889.

This, then, was the woman who took up the cudgels on behalf of the girls who endured the conditions of sweated labour in the match factory. She published articles under such titles as 'White Slavery in London'. She visited the girls, probed the facts, and encouraged them to stand out for their rights as human beings. Other newspapers took the matter up. A strike was organized and was astonishingly successful. All the modest demands of the girls were met. A Union was formed, with Annie Besant as Secretary, in order that the gains of the workers might be consolidated. The Webbs recorded their judgement in these words: 'The match girls' victory turned a new leaf in Trade Union Annals. . . . It was a new experience for the weak to succeed. . . . The lesson was not lost on the workers.'[3] Indeed it was not, as Dr Ann Stafford has clearly shown in her study of the causes of the great London Dock Strike of 1889 which marked a turning-point

[3] *History of Trade Unionism*, Beatrice & Sidney Webb (London, 1894).

in English history. 'The perspective of time enables us to understand the causes of the dock strike more clearly today; for though it appeared to contemporary writers to be an entirely new phenomenon, in fact a chain-reaction among the most helpless of London's workers had been started by the East-End Match Girls in 1888.'[4] These judgements reflect one of the ways in which the presence of women in industry increased their power in determining the course of events.

REPERCUSSIONS AMONG THE UPPER CLASSES

The growing economic independence of working-class women had its effect on their more privileged sisters of the upper classes who had nothing much to do in life but be paid for by the men who were the breadwinners and who expected them to be fashionable and obedient. It began to occur to some of these ladies of leisure that their poorer sisters had a measure of independence which was more desirable than their limited and artificial kind of existence. In more recent times, of course, the participation of women in two world wars, both as industrial workers, and as members of the combatant forces, has proved their indispensability in roles that had previously been regarded as reserved for men.

Another factor which has helped to alter the image of womanhood in the modern world is the active participation of women in athletics. The hallmark of a certain type of Victorian woman was a kind of self-induced sickness. It could have been rightly said that there was 'no health in them'. The coat of arms of the gentle-woman of that period might well have shown a bottle of smelling-salts in one corner and a female figure recumbent in another. As Irene Clephane has observed: 'This type of invalidism appeared not merely interesting but attractive:

[4] *A Match to Fire the Thames* (Hodder, 1961), p. 28.

it was almost the only way in which they could attract attention to themselves, while remaining models of propriety, in a world indifferent to their potential intellectual or athletic endowments.'[5] Of course there were many exceptions to this useless form of existence, even among the well-to-do, and many women, such as Hannah More, undertook a wide variety of philanthropic work, and engaged in intellectual activity. A great gulf divided many of the 'ladies of distinction', however, from the working women such as those who walked every year from Wales to London in search of seasonal employment. Nowadays the ladies of distinction are those who, like the celebrated Dr Barbara Moore, walk from one end of Britain to the other, or otherwise excel in feats of endurance as demanding as any man would dare to face.

EQUALITY BEFORE THE LAW

A series of legal enactments from 1870 onwards have resulted in our discarding completely the idea that husband and wife are one person in law. Before the Married Women's Property Acts of the late Victorian period a married woman owned no property. Her husband could say with legal exactitude: 'What's yours is mine and what's mine is my own.' Although at the marriage service he might say 'with all my worldly goods I thee endow', it was really the other way round. The position of the married woman before the law today is very different from what it was a hundred years ago. Then, according to Sir William Blackstone, the very being or legal existence of a woman was suspended during her marriage.

EDUCATION

The battle for equal educational opportunities at the elementary and secondary level had been largely won

[5] *Towards Sex Freedom* (John Lane, 1935).

by the end of the last century. The struggle for equality in higher education had been sterner and more prolonged. In spite of the fact that Girton College, Cambridge was opened in 1869, and Somerville College and Lady Margaret Hall, Oxford, in 1879, Britain's oldest universities have shown a conservative reluctance to recognize the capacities and the new status of women.

THE BATTLE FOR THE FRANCHISE

This chapter began with a reference to Emmeline Pankhurst. The name Pankhurst is indelibly associated with one aspect of the wide movement towards female emancipation—the securing of political enfranchisement for women. It is in many ways the most colourful part of the whole story. Mrs Pankhurst and her militant supporters captured the public imagination by their violent and spectacular methods. At a great meeting in the City of Bristol the then Prime Minister, Sir Henry Campbell-Bannerman rose to make a speech. He was, however, prevented from making himself heard by a booming feminine voice which repeatedly demanded 'Votes for Women'. This stentorian request came from an intrepid suffragette who had allowed herself to be lowered inside the large base pipe of the concert organ before proceedings began. Filing through the iron chains which women used to fasten themselves to the galleries in such meetings was child's play compared with the task of removing the offender from the bowels of the organ.

Such tactics inevitably called forth a variety of comments. Dean Inge, in a typically patrician pronouncement, says: 'Too much importance has been attributed to the noisy hooligans and hysterical or sexually inverted women who under cover of a legitimate political agitation brought disgrace upon their sex and country in the years before the Great War.'⁶ It is instructive to compare this slighting appraisal of the suffragettes with the words of Lord Pethick-Lawrence. Writing in the Preface to a book about the work of the Pankhursts and their supporters he says: 'No one reading the pages of this book ... can do so without a feeling of intense admiration for the courage and devotion shown by those who made heavy sacrifice for the cause. Health and freedom were given up, social ostracism was incurred. Each in his or her own way gave of their best, men and women, militants and constitutionalists. Some only of these have their names recorded here. Many more will have no written memorial. But they too were faithful in their testimony, and their lives are woven into the fabric of civilization.'⁷

The judgement of the noble Lord is certainly more perceptive than that of the Dean. It is, of course, undoubtedly true that the eventual victory of the women's cause owed much to those who quietly and persistently fought for their political rights by constitutional means. More than a century before the founding of the Women's Social and Political Union Mary Wollstonecraft had set out the wrongs of her fellow women in a book called *A Vindication of the Rights of Women*. Horace Walpole referred to her as 'a hyena in petticoats'. In 1825 William Thompson, a disciple of Robert Owen, wrote his *Appeal to one Half of the Human Race, Women, Against the Pretensions of the Other Half, Men*: a title which, whilst it can hardly be described as snappy, clearly indicates the theme. In 1867 John Stuart Mill attempted unsuccessfully to tack a suffrage amendment on to the Reform Bill.

Those who are still disposed to judge harshly the more militant feminists who pestered Members of Parliament, badgered Cabinet Ministers and threw stones at the

⁶ *Christian Ethics and Modern Problems*, p. 290.
⁷ *Unshackled*, Christabel Pankhurst (Hutchinson, 1959), p. 14.

windows of No. 10 Downing Street might, perhaps, remember the almost unbelievable intransigence of their male opponents who blocked the road to reform. In 1892, Mr Gladstone addressed a letter to Mr S. Smith, M.P., in which he explained his objection to Sir Albert Rollitt's Bill to extend parliamentary franchise to women. 'I have no fear', he wrote, 'lest the woman should encroach upon the power of the man. The fear I have is lest we should invite her unwittingly to trespass upon the delicacy, the purity, the refinement, the elevation of her own nature, which are the present source of its power.' For those who were determined to break down the ramparts of the bastion of male privilege, the high-sounding verbosity of the Grand Old Man must have been almost harder to bear than the often scurrilous attacks of their less gentlemanly opponents.

It was not until 1907 that women in England won the right to vote in municipal elections. In 1918 they were enfranchised, though the final impediments to completely equal voting rights with men were not removed till 1928 —thirty-four years after the women of New Zealand had been given the vote, twenty-six years behind Australia, twenty-one years behind Finland, fourteen years behind Iceland, and eleven years behind the U.S.S.R.

There is a note of sadness in the concluding chapters of the story of a struggle which at times convulsed the nation and called forth many a heroic sacrifice. When victory at last was won and women gained the vote the nation was exhausted by war and preoccupied with other things. 'Like some obliterating tempest the war seemed to impose oblivion on the years which preceded it. The curious observer picking his way back to those times before 1914 feels not unlike someone wandering over a fair-ground from which humanity has been driven to shelter by a sudden deluge. There lie the scraps of paper, the scattered

A TRUMPET VOICE SOUNDS 53

debris of gaiety—all the fun of the fair silent and sheeted. He can scarcely conceive it as it was, crowded with humanity, gay and brilliant; the stalls, garishly lighted, and tempting humanity with anything from flashing jewellery to pig's trotters: the men bawling their wares: the crash of the ball on the coconut: the boat-swings, rising and falling, filled with passengers laughing and screaming. . . .'[8]

The same note of sadness creeps into the moving account of the death of Mrs Emmeline Pankhurst by her daughter: 'She died as the day came, with her face to the morning sky. . . . The House of Lords passed the final measure of votes for women in the hour her body, which had suffered so much for the cause, was laid in the grave. She, who had come in their need, had stayed with the women as long as they still might need her, and then she went away.'[9]

THE UNITED NATIONS

In the years of its existence the United Nations Organization has turned its attention to the rights of women in a number of different ways. Its concern is reflected in the Universal Declaration of Human Rights adopted by the General Assembly in 1948, and in the Draft Convention on the Political Rights of Women adopted by the same Assembly in 1952. The Status of Women Commission of the United Nations has carefully studied the nationality and property rights of women.

THE ONGOING REVOLUTION

Of course the effort to achieve equal opportunities for women is made harder by the need to battle with long-established customs and to break through the

---

[8] *Votes for Women*, Roger Fulford (Faber, 1957), p. 306.
[9] *Unshackled*, Christabel Pankhurst, p. 299.

thought-barrier which we unconsciously erect to save us from the painful processes of adjustment to disturbing truths. Even when clear reasoning has shown their inadequacy, old traditions persist and often they prove, in the words of Virginia Woolf, to be 'tough as roots but intangible as sea-mist'. Moreover, it is not only men who resist progress. When new doors are opened women are themselves often reluctant to pass through to the fields of larger opportunity that lie on the other side. There are many understandable reasons for this, some of them bad and others good. There is in most of us, men and women alike, an inertia which accepts the status quo because it is easier to jog along with things as they are than to play our part in a revolution, however mild its methods. On the other hand, there are many women who are perfectly capable of playing a leading part in the political or commercial life of their country who are persuaded that they are rendering an even higher service in building and maintaining a home. To some of those who fought so hard for the political rights of women, and who bemoan the fact that more than forty years after the first woman M.P. took her seat in the House of Commons there are still less than thirty women in that Chamber, this apparent anticlimax may be a grievous disappointment. But the revolution continues. In the Western world its influence and results are more diffused. Elsewhere, as in the young nations on the African continent, the impact of Western ideas is rapidly transforming the pattern of sexual relationship and releasing woman from the limitation imposed upon her by male domination.

ALTERATIONS IN THE PATTERN OF DOMESTICITY

It is not always recognized that the changes affecting women have their repercussions on men. One way of looking at this is to say that the advance of Woman has been at the expense of Man. Such a view can only be held by those who still cling to the idea of the world as made for men, and who regard women as creatures relegated by the fact of their sex to an existence limited by well-defined boundaries. A more discerning view of the matter is that which recognizes that parallel with the fact of the emancipation of Woman is the liberation of Man from the old errors which have flourished in a world which he has dominated, and which have greatly impoverished the life of both sexes.

One important result of the whole movement which sets men and women in a new relationship is that the domestic pattern of home-life is changing. Particularly in America, many of the chores once performed almost exclusively by women are now being shared by the men. The care of children is increasingly the concern of the father who is often as competent at bathing the baby as his wife. The idea is spreading that, as the mother has to be present at the birth of her baby, the father should be there as well, not only because the child is also his, but because his presence can give to his wife the confidence and comfort she particularly needs at that time. We shall no doubt come to the point where we look back in amazement at the days when the husband was rigidly excluded from the presence of his wife when their child was being born.

THE 'WORKING WIFE'

The fact that men are playing a greater part in the life of the home is closely connected with the trend towards the greater employment of married women. There has been a steady increase in Britain over the past decade in the number of married women in gainful employment, regardless of the fact that the total number of women of working age (15-59) has declined in that period by about 100,000. The number of women in the working population increased by 920,000 between 1950 and 1960. In 1950 married women represented 41 per cent of all employed women; in 1960 they were over 52 per cent. Ministry of Labour returns for 1957 indicate that out of 12,820,000 married women in Britain nearly four million were gainfully employed.

Some of the facts about 'working wives' and about the attitudes of employers towards them have been studied in two papers written for the Institute of Personnel Management.[10] It is pointed out that the growth in the number of married women going out to work is the result of smaller families, the reduction in the amount of time which has to be spent on housework (owing to labour-saving devices), and the desire to improve the home and increase the standard of living. None of the women questioned about their motives revealed any feminist egalitarianism, militant or otherwise. The fact of sex equality is just accepted as is also its corollary that marriage should be a real partnership.

The attitude of employers of labour is, on the whole, rather less egalitarian. Viola Klein concludes the second of the two Reports to which reference has been made with these words: 'One is left with the general impression that in most firms the employment of married women is accepted as a necessary expedient to tide over a period of labour shortage. Few managements, other than those traditionally employing female labour in large numbers, have yet accepted the idea that married women workers have come to stay. Adjustments to fit them into the existing labour force are therefore mostly made *ad hoc* and are not part of a long-term labour policy. It will presumably need a longer period of full employment and industrial expansion before employers can be persuaded to regard

[10] *Working Wives* and *Employing Married Women,* both written by Viola Klein (1961).

married women as a substantial and useful part of their normal personnel, for whom working conditions will have to be created which will enable them to pull their full weight.'

Inequalities in the rates of pay as between men and women remain, though the situation is improving. Daniel Jenkins has warned us in a recent book that 'nothing is a greater over-simplification than the slogan "Equal pay for equal work",' and he suggests that 'while society, whether rightly or wrongly, expects men with family responsibilities to shoulder much heavier burdens than it does most women, it will always seem more reasonable that such men should be better paid than women doing similar work'.[11] It remains true, however, that in most spheres of work the discrepancies between the rates paid to men and women are an injustice to the women, and the attempt to remedy this situation must be maintained.

SOME CHRISTIAN REACTIONS

So far in this chapter we have been glancing at various aspects of that revolutionary movement which has advanced the position of woman in society and accorded her a place of influence and opportunity in spheres from which formerly she was largely excluded. We have noted that though men have played a conscious and not inconspicuous part in this movement, the new factor has been the degree to which women themselves have taken up the cudgels. This has meant, and will mean increasingly in the future, that the woman's viewpoint is heard and her insights contribute to our understanding of life. It is also fair comment that, though individual Christians, and even ministers of the gospel, have taken a leading part in the struggle to establish the rights of women, the movement did not originate within the Churches. Indeed in

[11] *Equality and Excellence* (SCM, 1961), p. 89.

facing this aspect of rapid social change the Churches have often displayed a characteristically conservative outlook. This is not surprising since, as we have seen, the Christian tradition has insisted, from the time of St Paul onwards, that the sexual order created by God places women in a subordinate position.

It is worthwhile quoting Dean Inge again to show the attitude of conservative reaction in its blandest form. Writing in 1930 he penned these words: 'Few can have observed recent developments without being convinced that the emancipation of women has reached a stage when it is a danger to society, or would be if it were not, after all, confined to a comparatively small class.'[12] Of course, 1930 is a long time ago, especially in regard to the revolution which we have under consideration. But it is not unusual to hear even in these days a comfortable Christian of the male sex asserting: 'We have given the women enough freedom; its time to call a halt.' Behind the use of the pronoun 'we' stand long centuries of androcentric thinking, and the native arrogance of the male who assumes always that he is by right the lord and master.

The Catholic Marriage Manual sets forth a point of view to which many Christians in non-Roman Churches would also doubtless subscribe. It says that God 'intended man to be the head and women the heart of the home. . . . Apart from anything God has to say explicitly about the matter, any study of male and female will teach us that man is best suited by nature to be the head, and women especially fitted to be the heart of the home. . . . St Paul was wiser than many people realize when he summed up the whole question in a few words: "Wives, obey your husbands; husbands, love your wives". Then comes the sugar to coat the pill: "One is not inferior

[12] *Christian Ethics and Modern Problems*, pp. 292-3.

to the other; each simply complements the other.'"[13]

This is, of course, a restatement of the traditional Christian belief about the roles of men and women. It is the attitude which was summed up by Tennyson when he wrote:

> *Man with the head and woman with the heart,*
> *Man to command and women to obey;*
> *All else confusion.*

Those lines were penned at a time when, apparently, even the sovereign on the throne had her doubts as to whether, being a woman, she had any right to be there. In a letter to her Uncle Leopold she confessed: 'I am every day more convinced that we women, if we are to be good women, feminine and amiable and domestic, are not fitted to reign.'[14] In these days, however, unless the reader has deliberately tried to close his mind to the significance of the events of the past century, the statement quoted from the *Catholic Marriage Manual* raises a host of questions. What is meant by man being the 'head' of the home, and woman its 'heart'? What is the evidence from 'nature' which suggests that the sexes are fitted for these roles? Why should wives obey their husbands unless they are in fact inferior at least in intellectual capacity and ability to make wise decisions?

THE CO-OPERATION OF MEN AND WOMEN IN THE CHURCHES

Happily there is evidence that these and similar questions are being asked, and that within the Christian Churches an attempt is being made to re-examine traditional beliefs regarding the relationship of men and women. Many

[13] *The Catholic Marriage Manual*, G. A. Kelly (Robert Hale, 1960), pp. 17, 18.
[14] *The Letters of Queen Victoria*, Vol. II, ed. by A. C. Benson and Viscount Esher, p. 444.

will regard it as unfortunate that the Church is driven to such a reappraisal of its position by the pressure of secular events. But if only we had not wandered so far from the wholeness of the Hebrew outlook we should put a big question mark by that phrase 'secular events'. We should believe that 'History is God's Workshop and time the roaring loom on which the garment of His Kingly rule is woven'. We should be more willing than sometimes we appear to be to recognize that God speaks through the onward march of events, and less dismayed when the new wine of revolutionary movements bursts the old wineskins of traditional concepts.

One important manifestation of concern about the relationship of men and women is the Department on the Co-operation of Men and Women in Church and Society of the World Council of Churches. The work of this Department originated under the title of 'The Commission on the Life and Work of Women in the Church'. The expansion of the work of that Commission and the deeper concept of its significance are reflected in the longer name now given to the Department. The Department's terms of reference were laid down at the Evanston Assembly of the W.C.C. in 1954. These included:

'Promoting among men and women the study of questions affecting the co-operation and the common services of men and women in the Churches and in society.

'Helping women to make their contribution to the total life of the Churches and urging the Churches to enable and stimulate women to share fully in the opportunities and responsibilities of Church membership.

'Fostering an ecumenical outlook in women's organizations in the various Churches and countries, and securing their participation in the ecumenical movement as a whole.'

During the comparatively short time of its existence this

Department has held a number of international consultations, each one devoted to a different aspect of the very wide subject which it keeps under review. For example, a consultation in Bossey in 1955 considered the place of professional women in the Church. Another gathering in Herrenalb in 1956 devoted itself to the theological aspects of men-women relationships. Each year an effort is made to establish closer contact with a different continent. Consultations at Ibadan and Nkongsamba in 1958 grappled with the particular problems of African women. The Department also seeks to co-operate with international organizations such as the United Nations Commission on the Status of Women.

Of course, there are severe limits to what such a Department can do, with a small staff, and facing, as it must do, the widest diversities of thought and practice within the countries and Churches which it serves. Nevertheless its work provides us with an important example of the way in which at the level of active inter-Church fellowship the ecumenical movement is taking an initiative which often sets it well in advance of what is happening within individual Churches. The value of this great movement is most vividly apparent at the level of practical work like that of refugee relief; but the provision of 'a service of thinking' is also of far-reaching importance. Ecumenical consultation can be a most exhausting, occasionally even a dispiriting business, but our labour is not in vain in the Lord if we are able to stimulate groups of keen Christians here and there among the Churches to begin to ask the right questions.

One example of the sort of question that very much needs to be asked is provided by the differing experiences in the Churches of what we may, perhaps, describe as fissiparous movements. In many Churches there are women's organizations and men's societies, existing in parallel, as integral parts of the Church structure. In the Methodist Church of Great Britain proposals are under consideration for the establishment of a men's movement, the purpose of which would be to draw more men into the fellowship of the Church. It is recognized that there is a great shortage of men in the Church and it is argued that men can be more easily drawn into an all-male fellowship than into one that is mixed.

Ought we to encourage one-sex societies in the Church? This is not an easy question to answer and its solution may well vary from one place to another. In some of the European Churches women have felt that they did not want separate women's organizations. They have in the past been accepted into the ministry and the higher functions of government in the Churches. In France women played an important part in the resistance movement, and they have served as ambassadors and in other official posts. But there has more recently been a tendency to replace women by men when filling vacancies in leading positions. Some women are feeling that perhaps they need their own feminine organizations in order to consolidate their position and advance their claim for equal status with men. In Asia the situation is different. More and more Churches are including women as their official representatives even when their quota is very small. This is very noticeable at international conferences.

There may be powerful arguments for one-sex organizations within the orbit of the Christian fellowship; but many of those which exist ought to be regarded as interim measures. One of the most important tasks before the Christian Church is that of helping men and women to explore the great questions about their relationship upon the answer to which depends the achieving of that wholeness of life in community which is God's intention for us all. It is quite obvious that such exploration requires that men and women should meet together. It is not enough that they should merely do so for the services of worship on Sunday; they must be encouraged to do so for those more informal occasions which the week-night meeting provides.

WOMEN IN THE CHRISTIAN MINISTRY

For reasons which many non-Christians—and even, one suspects, some faithful believers—find it difficult to understand, many Churches are still adamant in their refusal to ordain women to the Christian ministry. The opening to women of the doorway of the Upper House of the British Parliament was a painless operation compared with the difficulty of admitting women to some branches of the Christian ministry. The ramparts of priestly privilege have indeed been built 'firm and stout', and make the walls of Jericho look like papier-mâché. Nevertheless they will fall: the first breaches have been made. The Lutheran Churches of Norway, Denmark, Sweden, and Czechoslovakia ordain women to the ministry. In Germany the Lutherans have an order of '*Vikarinnen*'. They are trained in the same way as the men and are permitted to administer the Sacrament of Holy Communion. In Great Britain several of the Free Churches, including the Congregationalists and the Baptists, admit women to the ministry on equal terms with men.

The Methodist Church in Great Britain has reached an interesting point in its consideration of the question of accepting women into its ministry. Methodism has always given lay folk a large share in the life of the Church. John Wesley accepted women as lay preachers, albeit a little reluctantly at first, and prompted from behind by his remarkable mother, Susanna. In 1803 and again in 1835 the Methodist Conference pronounced preaching by women to be 'both unnecessary and generally undesired'. This led to a decline in their numbers.

At the time of Methodist union the practice of the uniting Churches varied and a committee was set up to discuss the admission of women to the ministry. In its report to the Conference of the United Church in 1933 it said 'we cannot find that there is any function of the ordained Ministry, as now exercised by men, for which a woman is disqualified by reason of her sex'. A committee appointed by the Methodist Conference in 1959 has confirmed this judgement. In the intervening years the matter has been discussed at several Conferences, and once again is now before the Methodist people in the form of a Report sent down for the consideration of the Districts and Circuits of the Church.

This Report is concerned not only with the question of admitting women to the ministry but also with the status of the Wesley Deaconesses. There are more than two hundred of these women giving full-time service to the Church. In some cases they are discharging most of the responsibilities of the ordained ministry, including that of administering the sacraments (by a dispensation covering the special requirements of the station to which the deaconness is appointed).

It is apparent that the considerations which have delayed the admission of women into the ministry of the Methodist Church in Great Britain are mainly practical rather than theological. Outstanding among these is the problem of the married woman minister who, unless she is to retire for a season, will have to face the difficulties of combining the claims of home and family with those of an itinerant ministry. As the Report of the 1959 Committee says: 'Because of the functional differences between husband and wife the ordination of a woman must carry implications that do not hold in the ordination of a man.' Such difficulties are real enough, and they are greater in the context of some ecclesiastical systems than in others.

But ecclesiastical systems themselves undergo change by the inexorable pressure of events.

One other factor which weighs with some of those Churches which have under consideration the question of the admission of women to the ministry is the possible repercussions of an affirmative decision upon the prospect of union with the Churches resolutely opposed to women ministers. Those specially entrusted with the painstaking work of exploring the thorny path towards the union of the Churches may be forgiven if they show the greatest reluctance to put one more stumbling-stone in the way of progress in that desirable direction. It is true of all warfare that advance on one front may be made at the price of a set-back on another. But happily the metaphor is not particularly apt, for in the matter of Church union it is not a case of opposing ecclesiastical armies, but of brethren making common cause against the enemy of schism. And so there is hope.

Of course, no one who is even faintly familiar with the facts will underestimate the difficulties that lie ahead. Conservative theologians may appear to be misguided to those of more liberal outlook, but they happen to believe that they are right. When a sincere man believes he is right he is likely to retreat only slowly when he moves at all. The typical conservative view is that our Lord appointed no woman to the company of the twelve, and His example should determine our practice. It is pointed out that the New Testament knows no women who served as elders, pastors or teachers, though some assisted. Moreover, the teaching about women keeping silence, since it is divinely inspired, must be taken seriously. It is argued by some that it is unfitting that woman, the author of life, should celebrate the sacrament of Christ's death.

In spite, however, of practical difficulties and theological objections there can be no doubt that the Christian ministry will increasingly open its ranks to women. If this is deemed to be an unwarranted prophecy the reply is that it is one that is being fulfilled as the very words are written. And the women who shrink from the very idea of seeing members of their own sex exercising the functions of the ministry may be reminded of the cocoon on the limb of a tree. Looking above it, it saw a beautiful butterfly sailing by and said: 'They'll never get me up in one of those things.'

THE NEED OF CHRISTIAN RESTATEMENT

In this chapter we have looked at some aspects of a revolution which has altered the position of women in Western society and is affecting the status of womanhood in a variety of ways all over the world. Even in the necessarily brief form in which the evidence is here presented it is an impressive record. Quite obviously we have been considering a factor in human development which undermines one of the consistent elements in the traditional teaching of the Church regarding the relationship of men and women. The doctrine of the headship of the male, asserted by St Paul and expounded by subsequent generations of Christian teachers, has been construed as the imposition of a divine order in sexual relationship in which women are subordinate to men. It is evident that women are no longer willing to be subordinate.

Rejection of the idea of inequality, however, can easily mean the loss of the important conception of order. Indeed, as we shall see in the next chapter, a careless assumption that we know what we mean by the equality of the sexes, can lead to an absence of order which is damaging to the well-being of society.

As an old and outmoded pattern of relationship passes away it is incumbent on all who care for the welfare of humanity to seek for that new pattern of order founded not on inequality but on equality. This involves the Christian in a fundamental task of theological rethinking. We shall return to this aspect of the matter in Chapter 7. But we must first continue our examination of those other factors of erosion which make such a critical reassessment of the Christian position even more urgently necessary.

CHAPTER FOUR

MELTING MORALITY?

THE MORAL delinquency of the present generation has become a painfully repetitive theme in books and newspaper articles. Many of these broadsides result from a combination of strong feeling and slender knowledge and call to mind Macaulay's comment on Moore's *Life of Byron*: 'We know of no spectacle so ridiculous as the British public in one of its periodical fits of morality.' Since this chapter is concerned with the subject of sexual morality it will be as well to begin with three warnings against the frequent errors which so often render a confused situation worse confounded.

THREE INITIAL WARNINGS

The first caveat is about statistics. These, unless they are treated with knowledge and care, can obscure rather than reveal the truth. False conclusions are often arrived at because comprehensive statistical data for one decade is set alongside incomplete figures for a comparable period a generation ago. The danger of being misled is particularly acute when an attempt is made to use statistics as the basis of moral comparisons.

One pertinent example is the way in which the divorce statistics are often handled by ill-informed people. Many factors must be borne in mind in examining these figures. The extension of the grounds of divorce by the passing of the Herbert Act in 1937; the granting of legal aid to those involved in divorce proceedings; the earlier average age of young people getting married; and the increased longevity of men and women—these are some of the reasons for the five-fold increase in the incidence of divorce between the middle 1930s and the late 1940s. Many other less discernible factors have been operative. It is never easy when dealing with the complexity of human behaviour and its motivations to be sure that all the evidence has been placed in the balances. In fact, it is impossible. And yet it is frequently assumed that the moral health of the nation has been assessed when a few figures have been flung on to a sheet of paper.

The second point is obvious enough, yet it cannot be made too often. It is that there is a perennial tendency for older people to criticize the younger generation. Of course, one generation is always different from another, and never was this more true than in this century of swift change. But if all the moral strictures which age has made upon youth could be added up it would seem a miracle that the world has not long since become a morass of corruption in which every flower of virtue has withered and died. This stigmatizing of one generation by another is one of the recurring absurdities of history. It is notoriously easy to forget what it was like to be young. Indeed, it is very difficult to believe that some older people were ever young at all. But harsh generalizations which proceed from lack of accurate knowledge and real understanding only serve to widen a gulf that we ought always to be trying to bridge. It is, of course, equally true that some young people are unsympathetic in their judgements about older folk. This is to be deplored, but there is perhaps more excuse. They have not lived long enough to grow wise. The pity of it is that before they grow out of the folly of youthful judgement on age they may fall into the absurdity of the old condemning the young. There is a particularly urgent need today for those who are able to build bridges of understanding between the generations.

Our final warning must be against the fallacy of

supposing that the overt behaviour of men and women, particularly in the sexual realm, is the only, or the most reliable, index of moral and spiritual health. It is true that Jesus said, 'You will recognize them by their fruits'; but the fruits of faith and disbelief are to be seen in attitudes as well as actions. There is in the teaching of Jesus the utmost stress on the importance of motivation. It is probably true that the majority of Christians in this country when they use the word immorality think of it mainly as denoting sexual misdemeanours. This indicates a perspective different from that revealed in the teaching of Jesus. If some sins are worse than others, as, of course, they are, then it is significant that the indignation of the Master burned more fiercely against the wickedness of hypocrisy than the shortcomings of a woman caught in an act of adultery.

If these warnings are based on a correct understanding of the situation then obviously we must proceed with some caution. The assertion, often made in these days, that we are witnessing a moral landslide, and that the very foundations of Christian morality are being swept away, must be tested against the facts, and the facts themselves must be seen, as far as possible, against the background of our times. And, anticipating a little the conclusion to which this chapter will come, as well as indicating the course to be followed: we shall endeavour to steer between the Scylla of apathy and the Charybdis of alarm.

We now proceed to examine some of the facts—sparse enough and hard to come by—which are germane to the present discussion.

HARD FACTS AND DIFFICULT CONCLUSIONS

(a) *The Illegitimacy Rate*

In Great Britain this has remained remarkably constant for the population as a whole over a prolonged period.

MELTING MORALITY? 71

From 1948 to 1958 it fluctuated between 14 and 15 illegitimate births per 10,000 women. In terms of percentages it was 6 per cent in 1870; 4·7 per cent in 1900; 4·8 per cent in 1930; 5·1 per cent in 1949; and 5 per cent in 1959.

There has been a trend towards earlier marriage and a corresponding tendency for unmarried mothers to be younger. In 1949, of every 10,000 girls aged 14 to 20, 37 had illegitimate babies; in 1958 the figure was 49. Conceptions among girls aged 12-17 numbered 30 in 10,000 in 1949, and 42 in 1958.

Of all girls getting married at 20 or under, 30 per cent were pregnant in 1948; in 1958 the percentage was 29. Of all the babies born to girls under 20 in 1948, 55 per cent were conceived out of wedlock; in 1958 the percentage was 52.

These figures raise a number of questions, not all of which can be answered with any degree of assurance. For example, how far can it be assumed that the so-called problem of teenage morals is largely connected with the proven fact that young people are maturing biologically much earlier than formerly? In 1858 the average age of first menstruation was 17 years; in 1950 it had fallen to 13·7 years. In spite of the tendency to marry earlier, this means that the interval between the time when sexual desire begins to be strongly felt and when it can be satisfied in marriage is longer. Again, is there not often considerable confusion in the adult mind when thinking of 'childhood'? This tends to be associated with the period of schooling. But we have been steadily advancing the school-leaving age and thus prolonging social childhood beyond physiological puberty. Would there not be something rather amusing, if it were not also pathetic, in the sight of so many older people being shocked at the evidence that teenagers have strong sexual feelings, and in these days are adopting the moral standards of their elders rather earlier than they did before the acceleration of their biological development?

(b) *Venereal Diseases*

Another cause of current concern in the field of sexual behaviour is the incidence of venereal diseases. The *British Journal of Venereal Diseases* published in December 1960 the results of an investigation. The figures from 148 clinics indicated that the incidence of gonorrhoea increased by 13·7 per cent between 1957 and 1958. The increase was most marked in the 18-19 year group—27·9 per cent in females and 36·3 per cent in males.

These figures led the Ministry of Health to say in its official Report for 1959:

'It seems likely that habitual promiscuity is more widespread than formerly. Medical Officers of Health, Doctors at Clinics for Venereal Diseases, Social Workers and others are especially anxious about sexual promiscuity among young people. . . . This is a matter which lies outside the immediate scope of preventive medicine but it is one of general concern about which everyone would like more information. . . . Though our society may seem to be physically and materially strong and healthy it is a matter for consideration whether its roots in family life may not be suffering from decay.'

Once again, however, to show that it is foolish to jump hastily to alarmist conclusions it must be noted that infection decreased among the 15 to 17 age group. It is perhaps important also to note that some observers believe that the increase is largely accounted for by immigration, particularly from the West Indies.

A report issued by the Birmingham Co-ordinating Committee for Coloured People in July 1961 indicated that while the number of new cases of syphilis treated in

Birmingham had fallen from 295 in 1950 to 129 in 1959, the corresponding figures for gonorrhoea were 462 and 1244. There is a strong implication that the three-fold increase in new cases of gonorrhoea is connected with the influx of coloured people and the overcrowded conditions in which they live. The Ministry of Health was wise in its 1960 report to stress the need for more research into the whole matter.

There are other considerations which indicate the need for the utmost caution in handling these statistics. What effect has the open encouragement to report the symptoms of venereal diseases had on the figures? Are there other factors affecting the spread of these diseases not directly related to the promiscuity which is, of course, almost the sole cause of contracting them? These questions are easy to ask—though it is noticeable that some writers never seem to ask them—but very difficult to answer.

Before leaving this part of the subject it may be of interest to note that in the past very great alarm has been expressed at the ravages of the venereal diseases. No doubt things were bad in 1913 but surely Christabel Pankhurst was guilty of wild exaggeration when she suggested that three-quarters of the male population suffered from VD. She wrote: 'For severely practical, common-sensible, sanitary reasons women are chary of marriage. When the best-informed and most experienced medical men say that the vast majority of men expose themselves before marriage to sexual disease, and that only an "insignificant minority", as one authority puts it—25 per cent at most—escape infection; when these medical authorities further say that sexual disease is difficult, if not impossible, to cure, healthy women naturally hesitate to marry. Mr Punch's "advice to those about to marry—Don't!" has a true and terrible application to the facts of the case.'[1]

[1] *The Great Scourge and How to End It*, pp. 99-100.

(c) *Crime*

There is at the present time a very great concern about the increase of crime in Britain. There is also evidence of a more thorough-going attempt on the part of the Government to deal with the problem than we have ever known before. Its general approach to the subject is admirably set forth in a White Paper.[2] There are now a great many research projects under the aegis of the Home Office as well as the major programme pursued by the Institute of Criminology at Cambridge University, under the direction of Professor Radzinowicz. Before coming to the matter of sexual offences a few more general comments will help us to see the wider picture.

The total number of indictable offences known to the police in England and Wales in 1938 was 283,220. In 1959, with an increase in the population of about 10 millions, the corresponding figure was 675,626. The figures refer to the serious crimes known to the police. The total number of persons found guilty of offences of all kinds in 1959 was 1,040,796. This number includes a variety of petty offences and it should be remembered that more than 48 per cent of all those convicted of any criminal charge in any court are guilty of offences relating to vehicles. Nevertheless the estimated value of property stolen in England and Wales in 1961 was £12,626,608.

It may seem easy to those who like to 'get together a few figures to illustrate next Sunday's sermon' to draw some 'obvious' conclusions from the criminal statistics. But, again, the note of caution needs to be sounded. In her lengthy study of *Social Science and Social Pathology*, Baroness Wootton says, 'That we should reject the official criminal statistics as evidence of criminal trends is hard doctrine, because it means that we must be content to

[2] *Penal Practice in a Changing Society* (H.M.S.O., 1960).

MELTING MORALITY? 75

confess ourselves quite ignorant as to whether our population is becoming more, or less, addicted to crime.'³ The most we can certainly say is that the figures reveal one or two features which are sufficiently persistent to justify the conclusion that they indicate the relative frequency of certain types of crime. Two outstanding facts are that crime is mainly a male occupation (the crime rate among men is more than seven times that among women); and that it is mainly the *young* male who breaks the law. The fact that the rate of convictions among young males between 14 and 17 years in 1955 was 1,603 for every 100,000, falling to 243 after the age of 30 indicates that law-breaking is, in the words of a German Criminologist 'an episode rather than a symptom'. This is in itself a hopeful fact.

Our particular concern is, of course, with sexual offences. The number of indictable sexual offences in 1955 was 5,408. The difficulties of making any sort of significant comparison with this figure are notorious. In a chapter on 'The Criminal Scene in the Past' Josephine Bell makes the following comment: 'Certainly at the turn of the century there were many fewer assaults reported, but the NSPCC and the RSPCA had not yet got into their stride and there were no public health officers making regular visits to individual houses, though religious missions existed in the poorer districts of big cities and brought to light many conditions that cried out for reform. It is perhaps significant that in 1900 in the police courts and at petty sessions dealing with minor crimes a very large number of men were convicted of "cruelty to a horse".... It seems very probably that a man who consistently underfed and beat his horse, who allowed its harness to chafe and neglected the resulting sore, would show a like brutality in his home towards his wife and

³ Allen & Unwin (1959), p. 25.

children, though their plight, unlike that of the horse, which was noticed in the street, never came before the courts. Wives, unless driven to extremes of misery, did not want to complain. Being knocked about by your husband was not at all respectable and no one must know of it. . . . Above all, no one must discover the sexual irregularities in the family. There must be no whisper of, no possible gossip over the wife's lover, the husband's mistress.'[4]

This is a discerning comment and pin-points one of the many factors which make criminal statistics an unreliable barometer for the measurement of morality. We must, however, take serious note of the fact that there has recently been a considerable increase in the offences which appear in the statistics as 'unlawful sexual intercourse with a girl under 13', and 'a similar offence where the girl is under 16'. In the case of the former the cases known to the police averaged 194 each year for the years 1950-54; and 285 for the year 1959; in the case of the latter the corresponding figures were 1,174 and 3,152. As far as teenagers were concerned the number found guilty of indictable sex offences in the age group 14-20 was 710 in 1938 and 1,829 in 1959.

The figures relating to prostitution offences show that the number of convictions in 1906 was 9,632. This number gradually decreased until in 1929 it was only 970. It then began to build up again until in 1955 it was 11,878. The passing of the Street Offences Act of 1959 has certainly driven the prostitutes from the streets, though it is doubtful whether it has had much effect on the amount of prostitution. The professional now uses different methods to attract her clients and advertises in various ways, even in special publications such as the *Ladies' Directory*, which was the subject of a recent successful prosecution. One effect of the new Act is that we shall be even more

[4] *Crime in our Time* (Nicholas Vane, 1962), p. 21.

dependent on speculation about the incidence of prostitution than we were before.

In 1954 the Government set up a Committee under the Chairmanship of Sir John Wolfenden to consider the law and practice relating to Homosexual Offences and Prostitution. Its Report was published in 1957. On the subject of homosexuality it had this to say: 'It is widely believed that the prevalence of homosexuality in this country has greatly increased during the past fifty years and that homosexual behaviour is much more frequent than used to be the case. It is certainly true that the whole subject of homosexuality is much more freely discussed today than it was formerly; but this is not in itself evidence that homosexuality is today more prevalent, or homosexual behaviour more widespread, than it was when mention of it was less common. Sexual matters in general are more openly talked about today than they were in the days of our parents and grandparents. . . . It is certainly true also that the number of homosexual offences known to the police has increased considerably. It does not, however, necessarily follow from these figures that there has been an increase either in homosexuality or in homosexual behaviour; still less can these figures be regarded as an infallible measure of any increase which may have occurred during that period.'[5] The Report goes on to point out that the methods adopted by the police and the intensity of their viligance vary greatly from time to time, and from place to place, and are affected by such factors as the ups and downs of public indignation aroused by much-publicized cases.

Further examination of the statistics relating to sexual offences would only lead to a wearisome reiteration of the point which is repeatedly emphasized by those who speak

[5] *Report of the Committee on Homosexual Offences and Prostitution*, Cmd. 247 (H.M.S.O., 1957), p. 19.

with authority. They confirm the validity of at least the first of the warnings with which this chapter began. The only justification for spending so long on this consideration of statistical data is that this is the arena in which so much public discussion takes place. Such debate is often sterile and inconclusive because the protagonists have their own fixed views and are able with fatal facility to find figures which seem to support them. Are we then to assume that in this welter of confusion we can make no clear judgements which are indisputable? By no means, for there are in fact a number of factors quite plainly affecting the attitudes of modern men and women to sexual matters. We are more likely to see their significance when we have abandoned the moralistic attitude which tries to denigrate one generation by comparing it with another. If we attempt to draw up any sort of a balance sheet we shall discover that there are entries to be made in both the credit and the debit columns.

FACTORS AFFECTING MODERN ATTITUDES

(a) *The Sexual Emancipation of Women*
This particular facet of woman's new-found freedom is clearly brought out by Professor William G. Cole: 'In the nineteenth century, the "good" woman was almost completely denied the experience of erotic pleasure. Western civilization as a whole permitted the uninhibited enjoyment of coitus to the prostitute, the mistress, or the loose chambermaid but not to the wife and mother, for whom sex was a burden to be borne, a necessary evil to be endured for the sake of one's duty to posterity. The divine curse upon Eve was extended so that women not only brought forth their children in sorrow but conceived them in sorrow as well. If a wife discovered by accident that sexual pleasure was not an exclusively male phenomenon she jeopardized her

standing in her husband's eyes if she betrayed her discovery.'⁶

Though there is probably some exaggeration in this paragraph of Professor Cole's there is certainly substance in the point he is making. There has been a great change in the attitude of both men and women to female sexuality. It is more widely understood that women have physical sexual desires and that indeed no marriage may be regarded as satisfactory unless the pleasure experienced in coition is mutual. It is no accident that in the marriage manuals which continue to appear in large numbers great stress is laid on the importance of sexual adjustment in marriage. There is a real danger that some young people may be misled into believing that the art of love is so difficult of attainment as to be beyond their capacity. It is certainly true that some married people suffer needlessly because they are obsessed with the necessity of achieving invariably that mutual orgasm which is the standard text-book ideal. They might be greatly helped by the assurance that there can be all kinds of variations in the so-called standard pattern which may be fully satisfying to the persons concerned. If the new situation imposes new strains it also offers the possibility of a greater mutuality in that intimacy which lies at the heart of all true marriage.

But the particular point of importance for us is the effect of the sexual emancipation of women on the double standard of morality that in the past has been the inevitable accompaniment of the assumption by men of their superiority over women. Whilst it would be difficult to discover a Christian author writing in praise of prostitution, it is only too easy to find a number who speak of it almost as a regrettable necessity, as if the prostitute were essential to the maintenance of a respectable society—in

⁶ *Sex in Christianity and Psychoanalysis* (Allen & Unwin, 1956), pp. 281-2.

Lecky's memorable phrase: 'The eternal priestess of humanity, blasted for the sins of the people.'

The situation today is different. It would be generally asserted in Britain, particularly by the younger generation, that what is sauce for the goose is sauce for the gander also. Granting that women have sexual desires as well as men, and recognizing that contraception has gone a long way towards eliminating the 'penalty' of undesired conceptions, just as medical resources are being used to fight VD, the road is obviously open to women who see no reason for not adopting the same standards of behaviour as men. This means the inevitable break-up of behaviour patterns which in the past the Church, and society generally, have helped to enforce.

(b) Freedom of Discussion

This point has already been remarked upon in the quotation from the Wolfenden Report above. It scarcely needs to be expounded at any length, save to point out again that there is both a credit and debit side to this account. There can surely be very few enlightened people who would want to turn back the hands of the clock, even if it were possible to recall the days when discussion of sex was furtive if not completely banned. In so far as the modern attitude reflects a reversal of that negative fear of physical sexuality which we have considered earlier, it is to be whole-heartedly welcomed. But it must be recognized that much of the free and open discussion of sexual matters is based on a very inadequate understanding of the facts.

The work of Dr Kinsey and public reaction to it may be taken as an example of the shallow nature of much popular discussion. The Kinsey *Reports on Sexual Behaviour in the Human Male and Female* revealed a high percentage of deviation from the accepted moral standards of society, or perhaps we should say what we have pretended were the accepted standards. This, however, is not the really disturbing feature. The more significant thing is the assumption so popular in some quarters, and implicit in the conclusions of Dr Kinsey and his associates, that moral standards should conform to actualities. On this view all sexual behaviour is seen as natural. This is naturalism carried to extremes for which there is no justification. Kinsey tends always to lose sight of the relational aspects of sex, and indeed scarcely seems to recognize their existence. Dr Reinhold Niebuhr criticizes what he calls Kinsey's 'absurd hedonism' in a contribution to a symposium: 'One has the suspicion that the crude physiological naturalism which governs Kinsey's inquiry is not so much a considered frame of reference as it is a scheme of thought into which he was betrayed by ignorance. He surveyed a given field of inquiry and found that sexual life was everywhere under disciplines and restraints which could not be understood from the standpoint of sexual life itself. He obscured or was ignorant of the dimensions of human history, from the understanding of which these restraints could be given some meaning. Even if one would be compelled to criticize their extreme rigour, one might suspect that in the field of sex, particularly, the morbid rigour of the law enforcer has a secret affinity with some of the forces which actuated the law violator. But Kinsey makes no room for responsible criticisms of extant moral codes and attitudes, due to the consistency of his hedonism, and his blindness to all the complexities of the relation of the sexual impulse to the institutions of civilization.'[7]

The benefits and the dangers of free discussion of sex are apparent. It should be equally clear that the responsibility of the informed Christian is not to attempt to stifle

[7] *An Analysis of the Kinsey Reports on Sexual Behaviour*, ed. D. P. Geddes (Frederick Muller, 1954), pp. 68-9.

such discussion, but to guide it to wise and informed judgements. He will not try to defend the negative and ill-founded aspects of Christian traditional teaching; but neither will he relinquish his hold on judgements and insights which are valid, however unpopular they may be.

(c) *The Influence of Scientific Humanism*
It would be difficult to exaggerate the effect on the mind of the community of the pioneer work of Sigmund Freud and of those who have come after him. Vast numbers of people who have probably never read a single page of any serious work on the subject not only employ something of the jargon of modern psychology, but have soaked up some of its basic ideas. Very often the public understanding of what reputable psychologists have said is extremely slender, and popular judgements are sometimes founded on bowdlerized and ill-digested accounts of the works of the masters.

One of the unfortunate results of this diffusion of barely understood psychological knowledge is that ideas are often accepted as 'scientific' and, therefore, indisputable, which are, in fact, the value judgements of fallible scientists. It is frequently supposed that the scientist is exclusively concerned with objective realities, that he assumes nothing, and rigidly refuses to allow any personal bias of his own to enter into consideration of the evidence on which his conclusions are based. This is, of course, a gross over-simplification. Whatever be the nature of the evidence under scrutiny the scientist is a human being, passing that evidence through the mill of his mind, and seeking its meaning. It is particularly true of those sciences, like psychology and the various disciplines of sociology, that they are concerned to set facts in a context of meaning and value. This is what Christian faith also seeks to do. But the typical approach of the more aggressive secular humanists, which dismisses Christian faith and the religious foundation of morality, is reflected in two paragraphs from an essay by Baroness Wootton: 'Traditionally in the Western Christian World the whole field of social pathology has long been permeated by religious ideas—by concepts of taboo, sin, punishment and atonement set in the supernatural framework of the Christian dogmas; whereas the Humanist's standards are earthly, in a broad sense utilitarian, and, where possible, scientific. In determining the foundations of morality and the ultimate objectives of social policy, the Humanist is concerned with man's happiness and welfare in this life alone, and with the development of each and every individual's maximum potentiality for the good life conceived in these terms. All arguments that are derived from religious dogmas, or that rest solely upon appeals to the Will of God, pass the Humanist completely by. Admittedly such phrases as "potentiality for the good life" are far from being precise terms, and can be shot to pieces by professional philosophers: but for practical purposes it is clear enough what they mean. Indeed, in the present state of the world, even if we did not go beyond the purely negative definition that the Humanist is against hunger, poverty, ignorance, cruelty and bloodshed, we should have a sufficient basis for social policy.

'So much for values. Meanwhile in the approach to his goals the Humanist looks to scientific investigation both to provide a measure of his success and to devise techniques for accelerating his progress. In one sphere after another —in the treatment of criminals, or in the selection of civil servants—he substitutes measurement for guesswork, objective recording for subjective judgement; and utilizes the knowledge thus gained to improve future performance.'[8]

[8] *The Humanist Frame*, ed. by Julian Huxley (Allen & Unwin, 1961), pp. 348-9.

It is quite clear that the scientific humanist is concerned with values, and, though the Christian must dissent from many of his conclusions, he gladly salutes the nobility of vision which often characterizes the writings of leaders of the humanist school. But when the humanist produces the gibe that the progress of man is directly related to the extent to which God and religion have been abandoned he betrays an ignorance of the evolutionary nature of Christian faith itself. The Christian recognizes that the source of all truth is God, but that truth is mediated through human minds and, therefore, is inevitably distorted. This applies as much to so-called 'religious truth' as to any other. This means that the Christian, like the scientist, is under the obligation of constantly restating his belief. If at the present time the particular challenge to attempt such restatement comes from the direction of the social sciences, then the Christian acknowledges that this is one of the means which God is using to reveal the ever larger dimensions of truth. God always has used what are called 'secular pressures' in this way. But very often the word secular acts as an iron curtain in the realm of thought and produces a dichotomy which hinders the pursuit of that truth, the very nature of which is wholeness.

The effect of humanistic thinking is particularly apparent in the impatient dismissal of what are said to be the obscurantist embargoes on sexual freedom laid down in the Church's code of morals. The humanist claim is that the standards of Christian morality are inimical to the human happiness after which he is striving. Part of the continuing responsibility of the Christian apologist is to demonstrate that the Christian standard of behaviour is the sure road to the achievement of the good life, both for individuals and society. In fulfilling this task he will be made aware of the errors which have distorted the truth in the Christian teaching about sex, but will also see more clearly, because of new knowledge, the validity of the essential insights of that teaching. There is a sense in which the Christian apologist fights on two fronts. He makes war on the errors which are discoverable in the fabric of Christian tradition; he also opposes the fallacies which can be detected in the thinking of humanistic philosophies.

One particular sphere in which there is need for a great deal of rethinking is that of the present debate about the meaning of responsibility. More and more, particularly in relation to anti-social behaviour which contravenes the criminal law, the plea of diminished responsibility is heard. The claim is made that the pressure of justice demands consideration not only of the objective facts regarding the guilt or innocence of the accused, but also of the degree of culpability. The extent to which a person may rightly be blamed for an action is affected by a variety of factors, hereditary and environmental. The mental state of an offender may have been such that he cannot really be held responsible for the action of which he was guilty. It is this approach which lies behind the penal reform movement. Increasingly the emphasis is on treatment and rehabilitation rather than punishment and retribution. The importance of this aspect of the influence of social science on our outlook is that it emphasizes the obligation to provide the sort of social conditions which are conducive to good citizenship. But its danger is the dissemination of the idea that no one can be held responsible for anything. It may be falsely assumed, and often is, that any kind of sexual licence is both explained and excused, if not positively justified by the claim, 'I was born over-sexed, and that's that'. There is a widespread belief that wild statements of this kind are justified by 'science', and consequently one of our major problems is how to induce an adequate sense of responsibility in those whose lack of it is damaging to the ordered life of our society.

(d) *The Law*

Reference has already been made to the trend in penal practice away from harsh, and often vindictive sanctions, towards less punitive measures which offer the hope of rehabilitating the offender. This trend is naturally reflected in changes in the law.

The British Parliament has in recent years concerned itself with the law relating to several kinds of sexual behaviour. The Wolfenden Report, referred to earlier in this chapter, made recommendations relating to both prostitution and homosexuality. The Street Offences Act of 1959 was the result of the Government's acceptance of the Wolfenden approach to the problem of solicitation for immoral purposes. Whilst it is true the law now provides for the imprisonment of a prostitute for repeated offences, the most important remedial aspect of the new legislation is that it endeavours to deter the young prostitute from pursuing her downward course before she has gone too far. The system of police warnings and the use of the moral welfare worker to help the first offender are designed to this end.

The Wolfenden Recommendations on homosexuality have not yet been implemented. The first of them—'That homosexual behaviour between consenting adults in private be no longer a criminal offence'—provoked a great storm of public controversy, and, incidentally, revealed as few such debates have done, the extent of irrational feeling on the subject in the minds of many people. Several authoritative ecclesiastical assemblies, however, including the Methodist Conference, gave their approval to these recommendations, and there can be no doubt that the movement is away from the inordinately harsh penalties which the present law imposes on men convicted of homosexual activity.

The Obscene Publications Act of 1959 was essentially a liberalizing measure. It resulted in part from the pressure brought to bear on the Government by authors and publishers following a number of prosecutions of reputable members of those professions for writing and selling allegedly obscene works. The difficulties of devising a satisfactory legal definition of obscenity are very great. The Act was generally welcomed by those who are concerned to maintain high standards of public taste and decency, but some of the results of its operation need to be carefully watched. The famous case of D. H. Lawrence's *Lady Chatterley's Lover* was won on the ground that it is a work of literary merit and cannot, therefore, be said to corrupt. It was obvious during the public discussion of this case that opinions differed widely both as to the literary merits of the work and the motives of the author. The really significant point, however, frequently overlooked by those engaging in debate on the subject, is that, whereas previously the law would not permit detailed descriptions of coition in the context of a romantic novel, now it does, if the defence can substantiate the claim that the book shows literary or artistic merit. There are many, by no means given to squeamish reticence, who will feel that there is good sense in a law which disallows what Lawrence attempted to do, partly because the convention of the privacy of coition is a good one, but also because less reputable works may get through the hole in the mesh made by Lady Chatterley. However debatable these points may be, it is quite evident, both from the passing of the Act, and the discussion of the famous case referred to, that the law reflects a much less inhibited public attitude to sexual matters than obtained fifty years ago.

We shall be referring later to conception control and to artificial human insemination. We may here briefly note that, with regard to the former, there is no law in Britain against the use of contraceptives. There are bylaws in operation in most areas forbidding the slot-machine sale of contraceptives in public places; but otherwise their sale is unrestricted. In the case of artificial human insemination the matter has recently been investigated by a Government Committee of Enquiry under the Chairmanship of Lord Feversham. This Committee recommended that A.I. should not be made the subject of criminal proceedings.

There is a subtle inter-play between the law and public opinion. The former is largely determined by, and in its turn helps to influence, the latter. Recent changes in the law reflect a more positive attitude to sex, and are to be welcomed. At the same time the danger of confusing freedom and licence is a real one, and not all the diffused results of legislative revision are beneficial.

(e) *The Effects of Affluence*

When Harold Macmillan informed the British public that they had 'never had it so good' there were few who could dispute the economic truth of the statement. Many, to their credit, felt an uneasy twinge of conscience as they reflected on the vast gulf dividing haves from have-nots. From the far side of that gulf we must appear to be fabulously wealthy. Of course, even in egalitarian Britain, some sections of the community are wealthier than others. Old-age pensioners have undoubtedly suffered most through rising prices. At the other end of the scale many young people between 15 and 25 years of age are better off in terms of disposable income than they are ever likely to be again.

One of the obvious results of this is the growth of the

teenage market. The following newspaper report is fascinating and significant: 'A month-long survey, starting on 1st May, will investigate the wardrobes of teenage girls in Britain to find out what proportion of the weekly pay packet goes on coats, sweaters, shoes, stockings, underwear, and frills and furbelows generally.

'How many girls wear nightdresses and how many sleep in pyjamas will be turned into "vital statistics" for the firms which make goods for Britain's 4,320,000 unmarried young people.

'Young girls starting work as typists can earn £7 to £10 a week. Some of their older sisters are in the £1,000 a year class as secretaries and the pocket money of many a teen-age boy could make his father envious.

'The survey will concentrate on 17 types of goods. But it also seeks to know how much time teenagers spend watching television—what sort of programmes they see—how many times a week they go to the cinema and to dances—how many read newspapers and magazines—and how many use public libraries or buy books of their own.

'The team of investigators will also ask about listening to existing commercial broadcasts received here.

'Men's clothes, cameras, cars, motor cycles, scooters and holidays are also in the lists.

'The survey is being organized by Market Investigations Ltd. In 1959 it conducted a survey which showed that 7,500,000 young people, aged 12 to 24, spent more than £1,000 millions a year.'[9]

The efforts of those who want to sell more goods and gadgets to the teenager are matched by the purveyors of literature and entertainment. At the present time a Government Committee under the Chairmanship of Sir Harry Pilkington is enquiring into the future of sound

[9] *Guardian*, 1st January 1962.

radio and television broadcasting. It has received a great many memoranda from interested parties. A considerable number of those documents refer to the effects, particularly on young people, of plays and features which over-emphasize sex and violence. There is also considerable public concern about the commercial pressures exercised by advertisers using television and other media. Such a concern is to be encouraged, though the difficulties of discovering any really reliable evidence about the connection between bad plays and dubious advertisements, and delinquent behaviour are much greater than some people imagine. We probably cannot go much farther than the general judgement contained in the concluding paragraph of the Introduction to a booklet on teenage morals: 'It is not necessary to be a Marxist to concede that in part at least the moral climate is conditioned by the economic process—which includes the varied engines of advertising and publicity. One of the great political issues of the next quarter of a century throughout the Western world may concern the mastery of these forces, how they are to be used within a free society, and the recognition in all sections of political opinion that the quality of life matters as well as the standards of living.'[10]

CONCLUSION

This chapter began with the observation that many people think of the present time as one of moral recession. An examination of some of the statistics commonly quoted in alarmist articles failed to yield any satisfactory basis for the unrelieved pessimism which frequently colours what is written, especially in so far as it refers to the younger generation. The three-fold caveat with which the chapter opened was proved to be an important reminder

[10] *Teenage Morals* (Councils and Education Press, 1961), p. 4.

of the difficulties involved in any attempt to base sweeping moral judgements on limited and inconclusive statistical data.

In the second part of the chapter we have glanced briefly at some of the factors, the broad effects of which are more easily discernible. From the Christian point of view those effects are a mixture of good and bad. The good results are associated with the influences which have tended to reveal and correct the negative emphases which we had cause to regret when surveying the traditional Christian teaching about sexual relationship. The bad results flow from the failure of some of the representatives of the disciplines of modern science to understand the validity of the positive elements in Christian teaching, and even more from the popular misrepresentations of the results of psychological and sociological studies which have issued in a confusion between real liberty and destructive licence.

The conclusion must be that the question mark which follows the title of this chapter is justified. The situation is neither as black as some sensational writers have claimed, nor as good as shallow optimists would like to pretend. We have, however, abundant reason for urging the necessity of a clear and positive presentation of the Christian view of sex and the moral standards which are implicit in that view.

CHAPTER FIVE

EFFECTS OF AN EXPLOSION

THE BOOK of Common Prayer sets forth the three causes for which matrimony was ordained:

'First, It was ordained for the procreation of children....

'Secondly, It was ordained for a remedy against sin, and to avoid fornication; that such persons as have not the gift of continence might marry, and keep themselves undefiled members of Christ's body.

'Thirdly, It was ordained for the mutual society, help and comfort, that the one ought to have of the other, both in prosperity and adversity.'

Whether or not the enumeration of these three clauses is intended to indicate a definite order of priority, there is no doubt about the fact that Christian tradition has maintained that the primary purpose of coition is generation. It has also been allowed, though often with some reluctance, that coition is permissible in marriage as a relief of the concupiscence of sinful Man. To these two purposes was added a third (which in some orders of Service for Matrimony is put first): 'the mutual society, help and comfort' of man and wife, or, as the Book of Congregational Worship puts it 'the Sacrament of human society, for the comfort and help of His children'.

The traditional view of marriage as primarily an institution for procreation is challenged by several factors in the modern world. The most spectacular of these is the explosive rate of population increase. This, like many of our large problems is a many-sided matter and full of complexity. In order that we may grasp the immensity of the issues involved we shall attempt an outline of the

EFFECTS OF AN EXPLOSION 93

salient features of the problem before taking special note of its effect on our thinking about the relationship of men and women.

FACTS AND FIGURES

The population of the world at the present time is estimated as 2,700,000,000. The number of people in the world has been increasing for a very long time and it has, in fact, taken many thousands of years for it to reach the present level. But now suddenly we are faced with the fact that this very large number will probably have doubled by the end of the century.

It is almost impossible for the ordinary person to grasp the significance of such astronomical figures. Various comparisons help a little. The present rate of increase, which is about 1·6 per cent per annum, means that we add on to the world's population each year almost the equivalent of the total population of the British Isles. The number of mouths to be fed goes up by about 120,000 a day, or 5,000 an hour, or 80 a minute. Between 1930 and 1960 world population increased by 900,000,000 which may be as much as three times the total number in the world in the time of Christ.

Another fact to notice is that the rate of increase is itself increasing. Every time the experts revise their calculations they discover that previously they erred on the side of under-statement.

One further feature of the situation is that the poorest countries are growing the quickest. The birthrate in South East Asia is 44 per thousand of the population compared with 18 per thousand in Western Europe.

CAUSES

There are a number of related causes of this fantastic proliferation of people. Far and away the most powerful cause is the spectacular decrease in the death rate, and, to a lesser degree, an increase in the birth rate, consequent upon the improvement of medical services and public health. We may take the Island of Mauritius in the Indian Ocean as a particularly vivid example of what is happening. There from 1936-40 the death rate per thousand averaged 28. This had fallen to 12 in 1958. The control of death-dealing diseases such as malaria and tuberculosis has gone a long way towards removing one of the 'natural checks' on population increase about which the Rev. T. R. Malthus, the 18th-century clergyman, had much to say. The result of better health has been an increase in fertility, and the birth rate in Mauritius has risen from 33 to 41 per thousand over the same period that has witnessed the rapid reduction in the death rate. As a result of this the population is rising by about 3 per cent per annum whereas before the last war the figure was 1 per cent. If these fertility rates continue, and the mortality rate is brought down to the levels at present pertaining in Western countries, the total population of Mauritius, which is now a little over 600,000, will be 3,000,000 by the year 2,000.

It is surely one of the bitter ironies of history that the magnificent fight against disease, and the sacrificial labours of those who have worked in the front lines of the battle against the scourges which have caused the premature death of countless millions, should result in our facing one of the most intractable problems the world has ever known.

CONSEQUENCES

The consequences of this new factor in our human situation are many and varied. Some of them are formidable to contemplate. There is the fact that the largest increases are among the coloured peoples. China adds twelve

EFFECTS OF AN EXPLOSION 95

millions a year to her population, and India almost five millions. Because of the 'rising tide of colour' the Europeans, like the Christians, become a dwindling minority in the world. Whereas in 1930 something like thirty per cent of the world's population were of European stock this is likely to have fallen to twenty per cent by the year 2,000. It may be that in the long run these facts will be of little consequence. In the short run, however, they are bound to affect both the relationships of coloured and white peoples and the rate of development in underdeveloped countries.

A second consequence of population increase is the exacerbation of the problems connected with the war on want. Although in theory the world could contain and support a much greater number of people than at the present inhabit it, in fact everything depends upon whether the new babies, who are all consumers, are also potential producers. Many of them are not, either because they will be sick and ailing, or because they will grow up in an economic situation in which mass unemployment is likely to remain a major problem for some time to come. So, as the queue increases at the world's pantry doors, the schemes to improve the supplies fail to keep pace with the demand. The spectre of famine is never far away in many parts of the world, and sometimes, as recently in China and Africa, it stalks through the land with results that horrify the world and leave the ordinary man with a feeling of impotence before the magnitude of the disaster and suffering revealed.

A third consequence of the rapid rise in the number of the world's tenants is that the risk of war is increased. It is sometimes suggested that the threat to peace comes from the poor countries where population pressures are keenly felt. It is, however, the richer countries whose power politics and tense nerves most obviously endanger our security. They have the resources to wage war and the means of obliterating civilization. But it is the competition of the great powers for the allegiance of the uncommitted countries that gives rise to situations which might well lead to disastrous conflict, and the poverty of many of those countries exposes them to the manœuvrings of the big powers who hope to win their support by offers of economic aid with strings attached.

SUGGESTED SOLUTIONS TO THE PROBLEM

It is a comparatively simple matter to outline the problem posed by the explosive rate of population increase. The real difficulties begin when we turn to a consideration of the ways in which the problem should be tackled. The weighing of one theory against another can be a fascinating business, and debates on the subject often provide a happy evening for all concerned, until, perhaps, someone rises to remind the company that during the hour and half they have spent together the population has increased by about 7,500. When it is also remembered that probably half the babies born in that period will die before their fifth birthday the underlying urgency of the situation is felt by all who are able to imagine even a little of the vast weight of human tragedy which the figures imply.

One thing is very clear: there is no single solution of the problem. Some writers have tended to oversimplify the issue by laying too much emphasis upon one particular theory. An example of this is to be found in a fascinating and informative study by a brilliant Brazilian nutritionist, Josué de Castro. Writing about hunger, he says: 'The crucial point of this essay is the argument that over-population does not cause starvation, but that starvation is the cause of over-population. This idea sounds paradoxical, since hunger, an agent of deterioration and death, seems unlikely to provoke an excessive increase in population. But in reality this is just what happens. Consider that the three countries that are held to be absolutely over-populated are China, India, and Japan; and it appears that the more these places are assailed by starvation the more the number of their inhabitants grows. . . . It is logical to deduce that although it is impossible to eradicate hunger by controlling the growth of population, it is perfectly possible to reverse the process and control the growth of population by doing away with starvation.'[1]

The thesis that lies behind this assertion is that human fertility varies in direct proportion as the protein content of the diet is increased or diminished. The argument is that the better the diet the lower the fertility. Dr de Castro drew up an impressive array of statistics in support of his contentions, but other experts have been able to show that there are big gaps in the argument. It is probably true that there is a real connection between diet and fertility, and undoubtedly the general lifting of the standard of living which usually accompanies improvements in food supplies is favourable to a lowering of the birth rate. But there is almost universal agreement that the major factor in the lowering of the birth rates in Western Countries is the deliberate practice of family limitation.

Of course, it goes without saying that quite apart from its effects upon fertility, it is part of our human duty to develop the resources of the earth for the benefit of all. Enormous reserves of potential wealth still remain untapped. It is estimated that between 17 and 18 thousand million acres of the world's land are cultivable, although only 3 thousand million acres are actually under cultivation. In addition there are 12 thousand million acres of desert which could be made fertile by the application of

[1] *The Geography of Hunger* (Gollancz, 1952), p. 31.

efficient methods of irrigation. Yet again, crop production could be vastly improved by the more widespread use of fertilizers, new varieties of seed, insecticides, and other more efficient methods of agricultural development. A Report issued by the Food and Agriculture Organization of the United Nations concluded that wheat production in India could be expanded by 30 per cent in ten years by these means. In Peru potato production has been more than doubled by a programme of teaching farmers to combat insects and diseases.

The bare statement of these facts is sufficient to demonstrate the particular responsibility of the wealthier nations towards the under-developed countries. The latter lack education and capital. Many commendable efforts have been made to provide assistance in both these regards, and at the present time there are welcome signs that the consciences of the Western nations are being more deeply stirred by the economic gulf separating them from those whose lot grows worse rather than better.

Another part of the problem is the conservatism and fatalism often encountered among those who have lived long in poverty and close to starvation. It is no easy task to stir people out of the kind of apathy engendered by long-continued misery, especially when they are entirely unfamiliar with even the simplest machinery. At the time of the Ground-nut Scheme there was a popular saying which reflected something of this difficulty: 'Give us the job and we will finish the tools.'

One other factor which can play some part in relieving population pressures is migration. It is not merely that the situation is made a little better by the movement of people from densely-populated to less-crowded areas; there is also the fact that those who come to live for a time in Western countries often return with knowledge and skills which enable them to help in the development of

EFFECTS OF AN EXPLOSION

their own countries. There are, of course, difficulties and many nations have imposed rigid restrictions on immigration. This very year the British Parliament, breaking with a long tradition of free entry of Commonwealth Citizens into the United Kingdom, has introduced restrictive legislation. Migration at best can only be regarded as a limited palliative.

It remains to mention the use of contraceptives to restrict the number of births. Various forms of contraception have, of course, been known and practised for a very long time. Some were extremely crude; others exceedingly peculiar. There is one ancient prophylactic against conception, the chief item in which is the swallowing of twenty-five live tadpoles. The modern 'pill', in spite of its present side-effects, is undoubtedly a great improvement both with regard to its efficacy, and, one imagines, its digestibility. The latter half of the 19th century, however, saw the first results of the application of more scientific methods of birth control (to use the rather incorrect description by which contraception has been popularly known). In 1877 Bradlaugh and Annie Besant were prosecuted for distributing a treatise on the subject entitled *The Fruits of Philosophy*, and alleged to be an obscene publication. Some years were to elapse before the matter was regarded as suitable for open discussion.

One of the important dates in the history of the development of an informed public opinion on the subject of contraception is the year 1918 which saw the publication of Dr Marie Stopes's *Married Love*. This book was the forerunner of a great number of marriage manuals, many of them well written and widely read. Dr Stopes's style will not suit everyone's taste today, but at the time her book was a brave and remarkable effort to break a conspiracy of silence and to set forth, in great detail, a view of the physical side of marriage which is realistic, romantic, and, in a very real sense, reverent. Moreover the author, recognizing that the happiness of many marriages was imperilled by the fear of unwanted pregnancies, set down detailed instructions regarding safe and hygienic methods of contraception.

In 1921 Dr Stopes used the proceeds from the very considerable sales of her book to open a birth control clinic in St Pancras. The hard-working women who ran a similar clinic opened shortly afterwards in Manchester were described by a hostile newspaper as 'the kind of women who visit matinées and sit with cigarettes between their painted lips'. The inheritor in Britain of these pioneering ventures is The Family Planning Association. With its more than 300 clinics throughout the land and its increasingly effective service to the community, it has become widely respected; clergymen sit on its committees and its President is a most distinguished member of the medical profession, recently created a baron. Those who have been long in the service of this Association must sometimes have difficulty in realizing that so many battles have been fought and won. It is possible that just now and then some of them utter a nostalgic sigh as they remember the excitement of past conflict which has now largely given way to the organizational responsibilities that rest upon a foundation of solid achievement.

The development of the birth control movement was, of course, well-advanced before the growth of public awareness of the population explosion. It is not surprising, therefore, that the use of scientific means of family limitation occupies an important place in the discussions about the policies to be adopted in order to deal with that problem.

THE IMPORTANCE OF PLANNED PARENTHOOD

Having looked very briefly at the general shape of the population problem we shall now be in a better position to appreciate the important judgement registered by a special Ecumenical Study Group which met at Mansfield College, Oxford, in April 1959. This was set up by the World Council of Churches and the International Missionary Council (which then had a separate existence),[2] and asked to consider 'Responsible Parenthood and the Population Problem'. Paragraph 6 of the Report of this Group says:

'We recognize the wide dimensions of the challenge, social, political, economic, medical and educational, and we welcome the fact that various agencies, national and international, are devoting their attention to them. Responsible parenthood does not in itself provide a solution to all problems of social and economic development, including the certainty of rapidly increasing world population. The application of science and technical progress in agriculture and industry and the maintenance of peace and international co-operation will have to play a major role. On the other hand, no acceptable solution seems in sight without responsibility taken by individual parents.'[3]

The importance of this judgement is that it signifies the emergence of a Protestant concensus in favour of responsible parenthood. The representatives of the Churches recognize that the population explosion presents us with a vast and many-sided problem. They acknowledge that it is a Christian duty to pursue the many possibilities of partial solutions which emerge from a study of the facts. But they are persuaded that the exercise of responsible parenthood is an indispensable part of any realistic attempt to grapple with the situation.

It is only fair to state that not all who have studied the

---

[2] The Two Councils were united at the New Delhi Assembly, 1961.
[3] This Report was first printed in the *Ecumenical Review*, Vol. XII, No. 1 (October 1959), and is now available as a separate document.

problem in detail are persuaded of the rightness of this judgement. Dr Kenneth Smith in a lengthy examination of various criticisms of the Malthusian theories has this to say: 'Alarm is felt at the growth of world population based on the same irrational foundations bequeathed to us by Malthus, but there is another view of the subject. While population is growing it shows there is room for it. If world population is growing it cannot be because food is short, it must be because longevity is increasing and health improving. A population whose standards are below subsistence level must decline, in accordance with Malthus's first postulate, and if the world were really short of food, population could not grow: children would die in the cradle, and the rates of infant and adult mortality would increase—yet growth is what we observe. A growing population, instead of being a thing to deplore, is a sign that, for the time being at all events, conditions are easier and health is better. . . . It is right that man should look to the future and conserve resources, but the indices to watch are not the figures of population but the rates of mortality, and particularly those of infant mortality. A population which is reducing these must be improving, and the appropriate course of action is not that of starving or frightening people into celibacy, but the vigorous application of human ingenuity to improving medical science and applying it more widely, to stimulating productivity and all other things which are conducive to human welfare and happiness.'[4]

Dr Smith does well to remind us that in many respects the theories of Malthus have been shown to be inadequate, and, in some instances, ill-founded. But it is too simple and too optimistic a view to say that the situation will take care of itself if only we press forward with schemes to increase the production of food and other necessities.

[4] *The Malthusian Controversy* (Routledge & Kegan Paul, 1951), pp. 330-1.

EFFECTS OF AN EXPLOSION 103

These things indeed we must do, but not leave other things undone. Enthusiasm for one particular course of action must not blind us to the unprecedented rate of population increase, and to the regrettable truth that the situation grows worse rather than better for increasing numbers who live on the verge of starvation. There is no escaping the fact that 'The growth of population has reached such dimensions and speed that it cannot help winning in a straight race against production'.[5]

The stage is now set for an examination of the impact on Christian thinking of the facts which we have briefly reviewed.

THE POSITION OF THE CHURCHES

The Protestant Churches generally have recently been placed in debt to Dr Richard M. Fagley who, as the Executive Secretary of the Commission of the Churches on International Affairs, wrote a book entitled *The Population Explosion and Christian Responsibility*.[6] The second half of this important and useful volume is a survey of the attitudes of various religious groups to parenthood and family. Dr Fagley includes brief notes on Hinduism, Buddhism, and Islam, but is mainly concerned with the three main divisions of Christianity: Eastern Orthodoxy, Roman Catholicism and Protestantism.

(a) The Eastern Orthodox Church

The thought of Eastern Orthodoxy has been particularly influenced by the early fathers of the Church and some official Orthodox leaders have spoken out very strongly against the non-procreative use of coition. There is, however, among the Churches of this tradition nothing

---
[5] *The Human Sum*, ed. by C. H. Rolph (Heinemann, 1957). Chapter 1, by Julian Huxley, p. 18.
[6] Oxford University Press (1960).

comparable with the body of detailed and definitive doctrine which guides the pronouncements of the Roman Catholic Church. It seems likely that some time will elapse before the views of the Orthodox brethren on Christian responsibility in relation to the population question are developed in detail.

(b) The Roman Catholic Church

The situation in the Roman Catholic Church is different. As we noted earlier (in Chapter 2) the main outlines of Roman Catholic doctrine are to be found in Thomas Aquinas. He left unchanged Augustine's teaching that the only permissible form of family limitation is complete abstinence. The Roman Catholic view of marriage is concerned with ends, rights, blessings, and reasons.

The 'end' of marriage—that is, the purpose it was designed to serve—is clearly stated as procreation. Thus the Code of Canon Law of 1917 says: 'The primary end of marriage is the procreation and education of children; its secondary end is mutual aid and the allaying of concupiscence.'

The 'rights' of marriage are defined in a way which also lays stress on the primacy of procreation, as this phrase in the Canon Law makes plain: 'Each party gives and accepts a perpetual and exclusive right over the body, for acts which are of themselves suitable for the generation of children.'

Roman Catholic statements about the 'blessings' of marriage are equally orientated toward the unequalled good of children. The order enshrined in Augustine's description of the three goods is maintained: offspring, conjugal faith, and the sacrament.

The 'reasons' for marriage are the motives and intentions of the couple themselves, and here, it is true, the Roman Catechism gives first place to the community of man and wife. But on the whole Roman Catholic doctrine is heavily weighted in favour of the view that the desire to procreate alone justifies coition.

There was, however, some development during the nineteenth century towards the acceptance by papal authorities of periodic continence as a permissible method of family planning under certain conditions. This position was carefully stated by Pope Pius XI in one of the longest of his encyclicals, *casti connubii*, issued on 31st December 1930. After rehearsing the familiar arguments for conception control, he refuted them all with the assertion that 'the conjugal act is destined primarily by nature for the begetting of children'. The encyclical then goes on to say that the 'rhythm method' of control is legitimate in certain circumstances: 'Nor are those considered as acting against nature who in the married state use their right in the proper manner, although on account of natural reasons either of time or of certain defects, new life cannot be brought forth.'

Pope Pius XII made specific reference to this teaching when addressing the Italian Union of Midwives in October 1951. Referring to the procreative duty of married couples he said: 'Serious reasons, such as those found in the medical, eugenic, economic and social "indications", can exempt for a long time, perhaps even for the whole duration of the marriage, from this positive duty.' Later in the same year the Pope expressed the hope 'that science will succeed in providing this licit method with a sufficiently secure basis, and the most recent information seems to confirm such a hope'.

It is frequently argued by those who support the Roman Catholic viewpoint on this subject that contraception is to be condemned because it is 'artificial', whereas the use of the 'safe period' is 'natural'. If, however, the use of temperature charts and other devices to determine the date of ovulation have papal approval, are we not justified in asking whether these are not just as 'artificial' as contraceptives? As for the use of the term 'natural', in this context, it is a question-begging word. For the Christian, that is natural which conforms to God's will for Man. It would appear that the use of Steroids taken orally to correct menstrual irregularities is acceptable to Roman Catholic authorities. Since, however, the effect of these is to induce temporary sterility, thus making them a most effective contraceptive, and since also very few women experience an entirely regular cycle, it is difficult to see what difference there is in principle between the use of 'pills', and mechanical or chemical devices.

Now the Christian discovers the will of God by paying heed to the revelation in holy scripture, and by the use of reason informed and illuminated by the Holy Spirit. The new thinking which places a much greater emphasis on the relational aspect of sex is, in the judgement of many, the result of the work of that Spirit of Truth who is ever striving with men, to break the chains of past error, and reveal a larger view of the mind and purpose of God. Within the Protestant Churches there has emerged a new understanding of the relationship between the relational and the procreational purposes of coition which involves a break away from the traditional insistence on the primacy of the latter. From this point of view it appears that the use of the 'safe period' is 'unnatural' rather than 'natural' in that it ties men and women in the most intimate expression of their love to seasons dictated by the impersonal biological mechanisms which govern the menstrual cycle.

It is, perhaps, because some of the opponents of contraception have sensed the force of this argument that they tend now to rely on other means of sustaining the attack.

It is not infrequently suggested that contraception is the enemy of sanctity in marriage and that it encourages promiscuity among young people. The first assertion is an unfortunate reflection of that fear of physical sexuality, and the anxiety in case men and women should enjoy their relationship too much, which we have noted earlier. Moreover, it is an unjustifiable indictment of the responsible and integrated home-life of innumerable married couples who understand very fully that the right use of contraception demands a high standard of discipline and self-control. The second assertion that contraception encourages promiscuity, even if it is true, is beside the point. If there were no such thing as sex, there would be no promiscuity. No one, however, would wish to claim that this makes sex in itself evil, though the readers of this book may well feel that some Christians have given the impression that this is what they believed.

(c) The Protestant Churches

It is sometimes said that the Protestant Churches trim their sails to suit the wind that happens to be blowing, and that the change in their attitude to contraception is a case in point. In one sense, it is very much to be hoped that we do trim our sails to the wind. The wind of God's Spirit is often the wind of change. A Church that never changed its mind would inevitably be a dead Church, worshipping the myth of a fixed tradition embodying a final exposition of truth.

The gibe that the Churches change their doctrines because of external pressures is foolish because it overlooks the delicate interaction between theology and history. In fact, each helps to shape the other. There is, therefore, no need to apologize because a number of factors have combined to produce a Protestant concensus of opinion on the subject of planned parenthood different from the views expressed a generation ago. The most recent of these factors is the population explosion, though the existence of the birth-control movement had already initiated the great debate before this tremendous new development began to loom large in the minds of thinking Christians. The effects of economic depression, and the fact that the limitation of the number of children was so often a manifest expression of a deeper sense of parental responsibility rather than the reverse, played their part in moving the Protestant Churches away from an attitude of opposition to one of acceptance. It is interesting to compare and contrast the various Church pronouncements issued during the past quarter of a century and to observe the references to these various factors which have affected Christian thinking on the subject of responsible parenthood. There are, of course, a very large number of such statements. Some of the most impressive have come from comparatively small religious societies like the Quakers—always remarkably forward-looking in their social thinking. Other Churches have as yet no officially formulated view. But there is no doubt about the quite rapid emergence of a Protestant concensus of judgement. The movement of thought is reflected in the Anglican pronouncements emanating from successive Lambeth Conferences, and in the *Declaration of the Methodist Conference* which has recently been substantially revised. We may now, therefore, look at what these two Churches have said.

The Anglican Church, through its Moral Welfare Council, has given more thorough and systematic study to the questions relating to sex and marriage than any other Protestant Church. It is, therefore, of particular interest to note that, whilst the Lambeth Conference of 1908 condemned contraception as 'an evil which jeopardizes home life', and the Conference of 1920 reiterated this judgement, by 1930 the views of many of the bishops

EFFECTS OF AN EXPLOSION 109

had changed. In that year, by a majority vote of 193 to 67 they declared that 'where there is a clearly felt moral obligation to limit or avoid parenthood' complete abstinence is the 'primary and obvious method'. But the Conference also judged that if there is a morally sound reason for avoiding abstinence 'other methods may be used, provided that this is done in the light of... Christian principles'.

The 1930 Lambeth Conference had other things to say about sexual relationship generally. It asserted that coition has 'a value of its own' in marriage, for by it 'married love is enhanced and its character strengthened'. The bishops still maintained, however, that procreation is the primary purpose of sexual union.

If in 1930 there were signs of an increasing awareness of the need for a deeper theological re-examination of the various aspects of the relationship of men and women, there was at the Lambeth Conference of 1958 really significant evidence of development along these lines. In preparation for that Conference a document was prepared (by Committee V) entitled *The Family in Contemporary Society*. This Report reflects both the progress of theological thinking within the Anglican Communion and the effects on that thinking of the demographic background against which many sections of that great Church have to live. The absolute primacy of procreation is rejected and the importance of the relational significance of coition between man and wife is stressed. Contraception as a means of family planning is more openly and warmly approved, provided that the methods are 'admissible to the Christian conscience'.

Dr D. Sherwin Bailey has made a distinguished and notable contribution to this forward movement in Anglican theological thinking. Some of the points which he powerfully expounds in his larger works are succinctly stated in an Appendix to *The Family in Contemporary Society*:

'In human beings, coitus is more than a device for reproduction—it is a complex experience, the purposes of which may be described as conceptional and relational... The Prayer Book states that the "first cause" for which matrimony was ordained is "the procreation of children to be brought up in the fear and nurture of the Lord and to the praise of His Holy Name". There is sound reason for suggesting that the process of procreation which is begun at conception is not terminated at birth, for parenthood involves many years of creative work with the growing child before that degree of personal maturity is attained at which he becomes fully the human being God intended him to be. Interpreted in this wider sense, the procreative purpose of coitus is not limited therefore to the promotion of conception. Those relational acts of coitus between husband and wife which cement and deepen their love, relieve their physical and psychological sexual tensions, and contribute to their personal fulfilment and integration, have an effect which naturally overflows the bounds of the one flesh, so that such coitus is directly beneficial to the whole family. It cannot too strongly be stressed that the wellbeing of the family depends to a greater extent than has perhaps been recognized hitherto, on the well-being of the one flesh—and to that well-being regular coitus makes a profound contribution.'[7]

The first official reference to the subject of contraception in any British Methodist document is contained in *A Declaration of the Methodist Church on the Christian View of Marriage and the Family*. Section VI of this document, which was adopted by the Methodist Conference in 1939, is entitled 'Parenthood and Birth Control'. This section

[7] Published by SCM (1958), p. 226.

EFFECTS OF AN EXPLOSION 111

begins by stressing the obligation of parenthood. In taking note of declining birth rates in the great industrial nations of the West, the document observes that diverse motives have led to the deliberate limitation of progeny. Some of these motives, such as the desire to secure for children higher standards of comfort, education, and culture, are not to be condemned. On the other hand some of the motives spring from the selfish desire for amusement and luxuries which would have to be given up with the coming of children.

The second half of the 1939 Methodist Statement discusses the practice of contraception, and indicates that two views are held by Christians: 'To many Christians this use of artificial means to prevent conception is deeply repugnant; they believe it to be contrary to nature and to the spirit of the Christian religion. They hold that if, for sufficient reasons, the bearing of children is to be avoided, Christian husbands and wives will exercise self-control, and that in abstaining from sexual intercourse their love will suffer no loss in its expression. For such persons this is felt to be a complete answer to the question.

'Other Christians, however, incline to a contrary opinion. They believe that something is lacking in marriage, even as a spiritual union, when it is deprived of all physical intercourse. Sexual intercourse, therefore, being a part of the complete married life, they think that conception-control may be a gift of God, through science, for the better performance of the function of parenthood, and so for the good of the race. Already research, while eliminating harmful methods, has devised a technique which is bringing parenthood under conscious control. Married people have now, for the most part, the power to determine how many children they will have, and when. Mankind has gained a new mastery over its destiny, and the result may be a far-reaching social revolution, the consequences of which no one can foresee.'

No attempt is made to pass an unqualified judgement on these two contrasted views, but certain considerations are indicated which should influence Christian decision: 'On the one hand, it may be urged that contraceptive methods make it possible to relieve the nervous strain of inhibition otherwise intolerable, and to avoid the suffering and exhaustion of too-frequent pregnancy and childbearing. They may be so used as to secure offspring under conditions most favourable to health and strength. But, on the other hand, the moral consequences will be deplorable if contraception develops a sensual habit of mind and impairs self-control. It cannot be stated too strongly that the necessity for self-control does not disappear with marriage; there are circumstances and long periods in married life in which no method other than abstinence is right or possible. Conception-control commends itself more to the Christian judgement when it is associated, not with the negative purpose of the refusal of parenthood or the undue limitation of families, but with the positive aim of producing the healthiest family in the healthiest possible way. If Christian people feel that they have reason and need to resort to contraception, they should first take competent medical advice on the practice in its physical aspect. The State should make such advice available for all classes.'

At the time when this Statement was endorsed there were some who objected not only to the degree of its acceptance of contraceptive method, but also to the public discussion at the Church's Annual Assembly of what they believed to be an improper subject. From this vantage point in time it will no doubt appear to many that the 1939 acceptance of contraception was of a slightly grudging kind, but it must be remembered that, so far as

EFFECTS OF AN EXPLOSION 113

this matter is concerned, twenty-two years is a long time. Nothing more clearly demonstrates the movement of Christian thought than the fact that the 1961 Statement on Parenthood and Family Planning was approved by the Methodist Conference without a dissentient voice being raised. Since its publication it has been warmly received, particularly by those with special pastoral responsibilities in education for marriage.

The Statement not only refers to the domestic factors which should affect decision regarding family planning, such as concern for the material welfare of children and the importance of fellowship between brothers and sisters, but goes on to say: 'Other and wider considerations affecting the responsibility and obligation of parenthood must be taken into account. In particular the demographic situation in the modern world raises complicated questions of far-reaching importance. The motives which have led, particularly in the western world, to the limitation of families, are as diverse as the pressures which have affected our thought and judgement on the matter. Undoubtedly our attitudes are often determined more by the acceptance of generally prevailing customs than by a conscious attempt to analyse the factors which have shaped the custom. Increasingly, however, people are becoming aware of the magnitude of the problem of the current rapid increase in world population.

'The "population explosion" can be dated from about the year 1930 when a widespread decline in death rates began to occur. During the 30 years between 1930 and 1960 world population increased by about 900 millions, which is almost eighteen times the present total population of Great Britain. The present annual net increase has been calculated at 1·6 per cent, which means some 44 million more persons each year. This rapid rate of increase exacerbates the conditions of poverty and hunger in many parts of the world. The facts about the present situation and the trends affecting the future are proper subjects of Christian study and concern. These subjects are of great complexity and the research of the expert and the keen interest of the layman are both essential to the creation of an informed judgement in the Churches. A responsible approach to parenthood will take into account not only the welfare of the family unit but the wider good of society. Moreover, Christians who live in wealthier regions have a duty to help their neighbours in less developed lands towards conditions in which they can enjoy the freedom to exercise responsible parenthood for themselves.'

In dealing with the practice of contraception the Statement goes beyond the equivocal Declaration of 1939 and sets forth quite clear guidance for the Methodist people: 'Some Christians believe that the only legitimate means of conception-control is abstinence from intercourse when a child is not desired. The Methodist Church, however, believes that there are other permissible ways of preventing conception. Provided that the means employed are acceptable to both husband and wife and that, on the best evidence available, they do neither physical nor emotional harm, for the purpose of conception-control there is no moral distinction between the practice of continence and the use of estimated periods of infertility, or of artificial barriers to the meeting of sperm and ovum, or, indeed, of drugs which would, if made effective and safe, inhibit or control ovulation in a calculable way. The Conference declares that for Christian people the determining issues (in this as in all else) are moral and spiritual.

'It is important that the biblical and theological ground of the foregoing judgement should be understood. In the biblical revelation the relational and the procreative functions of sex are equally rooted in the creative purpose of God, and neither is subordinated to the other. Objections to any method of conception-control which directly hinders the possibility of procreation usually proceed from a failure to recognize this fact. Such objections are sometimes the result of a deeply-rooted suspicion and fear of physical sexuality. It is important to recognize that continence may frustrate the relational ends of marriage. Contraception, on the other hand, can assist both the relational and the procreative ends of marriage by promoting marital harmony and enabling parents to space their children.'

At the end of his review of the questions relating to the population explosion and Christian responsibility referred to earlier in this chapter, Dr Richard Fagley stresses the importance of the present movement towards a unified Protestant judgement as a means of overcoming the neglect of the demographic problem in Western and United Nations policy. This is a valid point. What we have particularly noted in our consideration of the matter is the extent to which awareness of the population explosion has acted as a powerful stimulant to that important rethinking of the Christian doctrine of sex and marriage which is gathering momentum at the present time.

CHAPTER SIX

SCIENTIFIC INVASION

THERE HAVE been occasions when the spokesmen of the Christian Church have displayed an ignorance of science which was, in the words of William Temple, 'so immense as to be distinguished'. Bishop Wilberforce's Oxford debate with T. H. Huxley on the subject of evolution was a singularly bad day's work so far as the reputation of the Church was concerned. It is not part of our purpose here to recall the familiar details of the story of how the friendly co-operation between the men of science and religion was broken. There is much to regret in the story of the bitter controversy of the nineteenth century. Often Christian leaders took up dogmatic positions from which the Church was bound in the end to retreat before the attack of those who were rapidly accumulating a vast mass of new knowledge concerning the physical universe and the nature of the creative processes. It should in fairness be remembered, however, that in the Darwinian dispute, not all the scientists were with Darwin, and not all the clerics were against him.

SCIENCE AND RELIGION

The situation is very different today. It would be idle to pretend that there is no tension between science and religion. We noticed, when discussing some of the factors affecting the moral climate, that many of the assumptions which Christians make are challenged by the newer branches of science known as the Social Sciences. In the chapter on the population explosion we observed the conservative reaction of many Christians in the early days of the birth control movement against scientific methods of contraception. Some of the arguments still used by the opponents of this method of family planning are reminiscent of the early objections to the use of anaesthetics to relieve the pains of childbirth—based on the dubious exegesis of biblical texts. On the whole, however, the tension between science and religion today tends to be much more creative.

It is true that the very complexity of the manifold disciplines of science is such that the layman cannot be expected to grasp more than a little of what scientists are saying. Moreover, as a distinguished predecessor in this lectureship remarked, 'the average Englishman' has an 'invaluable capacity for holding simultaneously two or more sets of mutually inconsistent opinions'.[1] But there are encouraging signs that many Christians have learned what is fundamental to the pursuit of truth, whether by men of science or religion: the humility which patiently probes the facts as they present themselves, and searches for their meaning.

The point we have just made is very clearly expressed in a sermon preached by the then Archbishop of York before the British Association at Liverpool in 1953. 'The Christian theologian', he said, 'is in complete agreement with the man of science when he asserts that the fundamental principle of all research work is unbending integrity, and that evidence must be followed to its logical conclusions however disagreeable they may be. The Christian must welcome truth from whatever quarter it comes, for his Lord is the Truth as well as the Way and the Life. A sound Christian theology insists that the love of truth is as important as the practice of truthfulness. It is deeply to be regretted that sometimes Christians have forgotten this and denounced new discoveries not because

[1] *Science and Modern Life*, Sir E. John Russell (Epworth Press, 1955), p. 16.

they were untrue, but because they feared they would be dangerous and unsettling to faith. The Christian ... has no right to reject them solely because their consequences may be disconcerting.'

Paul Tillich, who may be regarded as one of the really great modern leaders of Protestant theological thought, has an interesting chapter on Science and Theology in which he replies to an address in which Albert Einstein attacked the idea of a personal God. In dealing with the argument that this idea contradicts the scientific interpretation of nature, Tillich makes two methodological remarks: 'Firstly we can agree entirely with Einstein when he warns the theologians not to build their doctrines in the dark spots of scientific research. This was the bad method of some apologetic fanatics of nineteenth-century theology, but it never was the attitude of any great theologian. Theology, above all, must leave to science the description of the whole of objects and their interdependence in nature and history, in man and his world. And beyond this, theology must leave to philosophy the description of the structures and categories of being itself and of the *logos* in which being becomes manifest. Any interference of theology with these tasks of philosophy and science is destructive for theology itself.

'Secondly we must ask every critic of theology to deal with theology with the same fairness which is demanded from everyone who deals, for instance, with physics—namely, to attack the most advanced and not some obsolete forms of a discipline.'[2]

Professor Tillich goes on from this to indicate an idea of a Personal God which is not inconsistent with scientific or philosophical concepts.

From this brief reference to a general point of view which seeks a synthesis of religious belief and scientific

[2] *Theology of Culture* (Oxford University Press, 1959), p. 129.

SCIENTIFIC INVASION 119

knowledge we turn to an examination of certain aspects of the impact of science upon the Christian interpretation of sex. Our observations are limited to some of the ways in which scientific discovery has corrected old errors, and scientific invention provided us with new powers.

THE CORRECTION OF OLD ERRORS

(a) *Concerning Procreation*

Dr D. Sherwin Bailey in his study of the man-woman relationship refers to the way in which the discoveries of medical science have revealed the falsity of certain familiar contentions of Christian writers.[3] Before the discovery of the processes of female ovulation, for example, it was widely supposed that male semen was virtually human life in embryo. The woman received this precious deposit during coition and nurtured it during the period of gestation. According to this inaccurate account of procreation the male plays the primary part—an idea which fitted very neatly into the androcentric pattern of thinking which regarded the male as pre-eminent in all things. Even an elementary acquaintance with the facts about the biology of human reproduction is sufficient to dispel so lop-sided a notion. Biologically the roles of male and female in achieving conception are equal. The supposedly more important role of the male may not now, therefore, any longer be cited as evidence of his superior status.

(b) *Concerning Coition.*

Another instance of the same sort of confusion, arising from fundamental ignorance, is the philosophical argument that begins by defining a good act as one which is under the control of the human will, and proceeds to

[3] *The Man-Woman Relationship in Christian Thought* (Longmans, 1959), pp. 241-3.

condemn coition as evil because it is, at any rate in its climax, not subject to the control of the will. This would seem to be just as unreasonable as to condemn sneezing as immoral because it is essentially involuntary. The false conclusion again results from a failure to understand the mechanisms which God Himself has created in order that conception may occur. The naïve suggestion made by Augustine that in paradise the congress of the sexes would be calm and unaccompanied by gross animal excitements is the inevitable corollary of this mistaken idea. It would be amusing were it not for the fact that it reflects that fear of physical sexuality which has had such disastrous consequences in the lives of generations of men and women.

Of course, in citing these examples we ought not to think of our Christian Fathers as hopelessly ill-informed compared with the enlightened apostles of science. In fact they were using the data provided by such science as there was. The important point is that if we follow their example and make use of what later scientific investigation has revealed we are bound to reject some of their conclusions about human sexuality and its significance.

(c) Concerning Masturbation

It is unfortunately true that, even when new facts have been absorbed, the attitudes which accompanied old errors live on. It seems more than likely that the exaggerated reverence for semen accounts in part for the inordinate emphasis which in the past has been put on the evil of male masturbation. It has been asserted that the practice results in insanity, disease, physical lassitude, and impotence. A great deal of what used to be said is undiluted nonsense, and the dire threats of well-intentioned (one hopes) but ignorant people must have done immensely more harm than the habit itself. Modern parents and teachers recognize that there is little to worry about except where masturbation becomes a fixed habit indicative of a neurosis. Even then fierce condemnation will do more harm than good.

(*d*) *Concerning Homosexuality*
It also seems probable that the particularly heavy penalties which the law prescribes for male homosexual activities are not unconnected with the old fallacy regarding the nature of semen. At the present time English law applies sanctions against men convicted of private homosexual acts with adults but not against women guilty of similar behaviour. Interestingly enough, in the case of prostitution offences it is the woman who is more harshly treated. The reason for this is that it is usually (though not always) the women who commit the offence of solicitation. In the case of homosexual activity, however, the discrimination between men and women has no clear explanation, and is evidently based upon an irrationality which is rooted in past error. Those who favour the introduction of more enlightened legislation on homosexual behaviour are very much aware of the illogical ferocity with which their appeal for a rational approach to the question is sometimes attacked. The roots of human error run deep.

(*e*) *Concerning Bisexuality*
It is interesting to note that present discussion of the causes and treatment of homosexuality sheds some light on the concept of bisexuality, which in its various forms, has a long history. It is still popularly believed that 'there is a bit of the man in every woman, and something of the woman in every man'. If pressed to provide the evidence for this assertion, many would probably point to the fact that some men are particularly gentle (the assumption

being that gentleness is a feminine characteristic), while some women are extremely tough (the assumption being that toughness is a male quality). On this slender basis extraordinary claims have been made. For example, it has been suggested that homosexuality is an in-born condition and arises from the fact that a person has had the misfortune to be so constituted that the sexual balance has come down rather too heavily on the wrong side. Or again, amateur theologians have even rushed in with the claim that the bisexuality of Jesus makes Him the Saviour of both men and women.

Amidst all this jungle of loose assertions, often accompanied by extreme dogmatism and an entire lack of any serious supporting evidence, a path is gradually being cleared. Dr Clifford Allen who has given more than a quarter of a century of study to problems of sexual abnormality says: 'We can state with confidence that there is no discernible difference between the physique of the homosexual and heterosexual by any tests, microscopical, biochemical, or endocrine of which we are aware at present.'[4] Dr D. J. West similarly concludes that 'the glandular theory of inversion has little to commend it'.[5]

This judgement is of particular importance in its indication of the possible methods of treating homosexuality. The injection of male hormones in a deviant may increase rather than cure his perverse sexual behaviour.

The examination of the theory of bisexuality, however, is not merely of interest to those who are concerned about the causes and treatment of homosexuality. The truth about the real nature of masculinity and femininity is of importance for a right understanding of the proper relationship of men and women.

[4] *Homosexuality* (Staples, 1958), p. 43.
[5] *Homosexuality* (Duckworth, 1955), p. 61.

There are, in fact, a bewildering variety of theories about what constitutes femininity and masculinity.[6] The line of development in thinking seems to pass through three stages. In the first woman is denied a soul, and femininity, as in the teaching of Aristotle, is a 'kind of natural defectiveness'. Then there comes the idea that woman is the reverse of man. More recently it has been urged that the association of psychological traits with sex is accidental rather than based on constitutional facts.

This last suggestion is very fully developed in the works of Margaret Mead, the famous anthropologist.[7] In a lengthy consideration of the subject she begins by asking the question: 'How are men and women to think about their maleness and their femaleness in this twentieth century, in which so many of our old ideas must be made new?' She then draws on her experience of seven South Sea Cultures to show how the differences and similarities in the bodies of human beings are the basis on which all our learnings about our sex and our relationship with the other sex are built. Dr Mead illustrates the fact that though everywhere there is patterning of sex roles, the patterns vary enormously from one culture to another. Quite obviously a great deal of what we think of as either typically masculine or characteristically feminine is the result of social stereotyping—of those age-old processes of education which have associated certain patterns of behaviour with men and others with women. This is why when we move from one culture to another we often discover that some of the characteristics we think of as 'masculine' are associated with women rather than men, and similarly men play a 'feminine' role. It is also true that there are very great differences within both sexes.

[6] See *The Feminine Character*, by Viola Klein, for a summary of the conclusions of a number of authoritative writers.
[7] *Male and Female* (Gollancz, 1949).

The importance of the searching questions raised by Margaret Mead and others should be obvious. She warns us against the mistake of trying to get rid of sex differences because thereby we abolish diversification as a contribution to the life of the community. We must persist with the new sort of question we are asking about the deep differences between men and women if we are to explore the richer significance of sex in terms of relationship. To many of our questions we may as yet find no satisfactory answer, but we must take advantage of all the new knowledge which helps us even if its main effect is painfully to shatter cherished ideas and superficial confidence. As we saw earlier the roles of men and women are undergoing rapid change in our own society.[8] We shall be wise to heed three assertions which Professor Mead makes in the last chapter of her book:

'To the extent that either sex is disadvantaged, the whole culture is poorer.'[9]

'When an activity to which each could have contributed —and probably all complex activities belong in this class —is limited to one sex, a rich differentiated quality is lost from the activity itself.'[10]

'We can build a whole society only by using both the gifts special to each sex and those shared by both sexes— by using the gifts of the whole of humanity.'[11]

(f) Concerning the Natural Powers of Men and Women

It is often asserted that men are stronger than women. This belief is partially responsible for the traditional assumption of male superiority. The assertion, however, is not as easily substantiated as might be expected. It is true that, generally speaking, men have greater muscular strength than women, though it is debatable how far this

---

[8] Pages 61-2. [9] *Male and Female*, p. 368. [10] Ibid. p. 374.
[11] Ibid. p. 384.

is due to the roles which society has assigned to men and women. Obviously individual women are capable, especially when specifically trained, of very impressive muscular feats. From earliest days women have, by reason of their biological function, been tied more closely than men to home and hearth. It is equally true that men acquired a greater variety of skills and experiences as a result of their hunting activities.

But strength is of various kinds. The confident assertion that men are stronger than women can soon be made to look nonsensical when other facts are taken into consideration. We now know, and there are statistics to prove it, that in almost every part of the world life expectancy is higher for women than for men. It is also common knowledge that, although more boys are born than girls, the survival rate among the latter is higher than among the former.

If we turn to those aspects of strength and weakness which are less easily measured, it is instructive that there are many indications that women are on the whole emotionally more resilient than men. They bend more easily before the winds of feeling, so often survive when men snap. This is not unconnected with the fact that the suicide rate is higher among men than women.[12]

These are some of the more obvious ways in which the less prejudiced approach demanded by scientific enquiry and research reveals the inadequacy, even the falsity, of some traditional assumptions. In spite of this, people will often insist on believing what they want to believe. Scientific enquiry itself can often produce results which are misleading, as, for example, when it was demonstrated that the average weight of the male brain (just over 3

---

[12] Louis Dublin and Bessie Bunzel in their study of suicide, *To Be or Not to Be* (1933), found that in U.S.A. the suicide rate was in the ratio of ten males to three females.

pounds) is about 4 ounces heavier than that of the female. This was taken as a clear indication of the superior intellectual powers of the man until it was also shown that there is no direct relation between the weight of the brain and intelligence.

It is, perhaps, unnecessary to add that the fact that men have excelled in most things in greater numbers than women is exactly what one would expect in a world where, speaking generally, women have been denied many of the opportunities claimed by men as their natural right.

THE PROVISION OF NEW POWERS

Having glanced at some of the ways in which old errors in understanding and interpretation are corrected by newer knowledge, we must now observe the manner in which applied science is invading the realm of human intimacy connected with conception and birth. This carries us into a fascinating field. Because of the complexity of the issues raised, and because we are dealing largely with situations for which there is no precedent, some of our conclusions must be tentative.

(a) Contraception

In the preceding chapter we noted the emergence of a Protestant concensus of opinion in favour of contraception as a means of family planning. We found that this developing judgement had been assisted both by economic and social pressures, of which the most notable was the explosive rate of population increase, as well as by the movement of theological thought concerning the nature of marriage and the purpose of sex.

What now concerns us is the fact that the provision and availability of effective contraceptives give to human beings a distinct measure of control over what was once regarded as God's prerogative. Whilst it has been part of the Church's traditional teaching that men and women are called to co-operate with the divine will in the great task of creation, it has been assumed that the number of off-spring born to a couple was a matter for the Lord to decide. This indeed is still substantially the teaching of the Roman Catholic Church which encourages its members to propagate children freely: 'The modern Catholic couple must be reminded that parenthood is the business of marriage. . . . The control of births, therefore, should always be the exceptional situation in marriage, never the normal.'[13] If there are valid reasons for limiting the number of children, married people must either abstain or make use of the 'safe period'. In the latter case, of course, whilst the chances of conception are reduced they are not entirely obviated. Among those who reject the Roman Catholic teaching, however, contraception is regarded, like many other products of science, as a gift of God, increasing both man's powers of decision and his responsibility to use those powers in conformity with the Divine purpose.

In relation to contraception, then, the main principle, for those who accept it, has been established. There will be many interesting developments in contraceptive techniques—the improvement in oral contraceptives which control or inhibit ovulation in a calculable way is likely to be very rapid—but providing they are acceptable to husband and wife, and do neither emotional nor physical harm, the principle will remain unaffected.

(b) Sterilization

Christian opinion has drawn a clear distinction between the prevention of conception as a means of family limitation, and the use of abortion for the same purpose. The latter is condemned both because it involves the destruction

---

[13] *The Catholic Marriage Manual*, G. A. Kelly (Robert Hale, 1960), p. 52.

of human life and because it imperils the life of the mother. (We are not here concerned with the question of therapeutic abortion and the state of the law relating to it.) Recently, however, there has been renewed discussion of the circumstances in which the operation for sterilization might be performed. A committee was set up by the Church of England Board for Social Responsibility in response to requests for guidance from Christian doctors in India about the propriety of their participation in their country's effort to ward off the threat of overpopulation by means which include the voluntary sterilization of men and women.

Traditionally, the Christian Church has condemned sterilization, whether compulsory or voluntary, not only on the ground that it involves mutilation of the human body, which is not a man's own to do with as he likes, but also because it deprives the person concerned of one of his most important endowments, the faculty of procreation. To this law there is only one exception, referred to by St Thomas Aquinas: 'If, however, the member be decayed and therefore a source of corruption to the whole body, then it is lawful with the consent of the owner of the member, to cut away the member for the welfare of the whole body, since each one is entrusted with the care of his own welfare. The same applies if it be done with the consent of the person whose business it is to care for the welfare of the person who has a decayed member; otherwise it is altogether unlawful to maim anyone.'[14]

The reference in this quotation is, of course, to castration, which is not now employed as a means of sterilization because its effects, which are irreversible, include alterations of secondary sexual characteristics. The means most commonly employed today are salpingectomy for

[14] *Summa Theologica*, II.II.14 (London, 1929).

SCIENTIFIC INVASION 129

the female, and vasectomy for the male. The former prevents the possibility of conception by severing and tying the Fallopian tubes between the ovaries and the uterus; the latter by dividing the *vas deferens* on each side of the groin, thus cutting off a portion of the seminal fluid and making it sterile. In the case of women, in spite of attempts to reverse the process, it is still generally regarded as irreversible. In the case of men, however, recent experiments in India suggest that it is possible, with some degree of success, to restore fertility in those on whom the operation of vasectomy has been performed.

The 1961 Annual Report of the Medical Defence Union prints an article on the legal position relating to sterilization in England. On the basis of opinions expressed by English and Scottish Counsel this may be briefly summarized by saying that sterilization on therapeutic or well-founded eugenic grounds would be upheld by the Court; but that it might not be upheld if the ground were merely that of personal convenience; and that it would most probably be condemned if there was a clear element of moral turpitude, damaging to the public interest (e.g. sterilization of a prostitute to enable her more conveniently to ply her trade).

The Church of England Committee took note of the fact that the question of sterilization had previously been considered in 1949-50.[15] Then the Committee was unable unreservedly either to commend or condemn sterilization as a means of population control. Two other facts had also to be taken into consideration. One was that the 1949-50 committee had been influenced by the impression that the process was irreversible; the other was the strong affirmation by the 1958 Lambeth Conference of the parental obligation of regulating the size

[15] See *Human Sterilization: Some Principles of Christian Ethics* (Church Information Board, 1951).

of the family, derived as much from Christian understanding of marriage and parenthood as from the social necessity of restraining population increase.

In the light of its consideration of the appeal for advice from the Indian doctors, the committee, speaking, of course, on its own authority, concluded:

'Faced as we are by a situation in which a responsible government is pursuing, together with other ameliorative measures, a policy of persuasion for voluntary sterilization, and asked by Christian doctors and nurses involved in the carrying out of this policy for help in deciding for themselves how far they can co-operate, we are bound to conclude that we find no grounds on which to reply in terms of an absolute negative. The Church of England does not claim to be infallible, and it may err. But it does believe in progressive revelation under the guidance of the Holy Spirit. And we believe that light on this question is slowly dawning. . . .'[16]

The committee gave less detailed consideration to sterilization for purposes other than that of population control. It found no place for compulsory sterilization, imposed either penally, or for the protection of society, or for the genetic improvement of the race. In the various cases which come under the heading of 'therapeutic sterilization' it is suggested that the case against the practice hardens at every step in the gradation from 'necessity' (as where the life of the mother would be placed in jeopardy if she conceived) to mere convenience. In discussing 'eugenic sterilization' the committee points out that since genetically determined abnormalities are now rapidly entering the treatable field, the indications for a practically irreversible operation for sterilization are to that extent diminished.

[16] *Sterilization: An Ethical Enquiry* (Church Information Office, 1962), p. 25.

(c) *Artificial Human Insemination*
The various techniques for the prevention of conception, however, are only one aspect of the new powers which science has vouchsafed to men and women respecting their procreative functions. Artificial human insemination is another modern technique[17] which has presented the Christian conscience with a complex of questions, many of which admit of no easy answer.

The practice of AIH (artificial insemination by husband) raises questions different from the ones posed by the practice of AID (artificial insemination by donor). Various Church pronouncements have been made indicating a judgement in favour of AIH in those cases where conception is prevented by malformation or other abnormality. Thus the Methodist Conference stated in 1958:

'The use of AIH does not raise the serious questions involved in the practice of AID and circumstances can arise in which there can be no moral objection to it.'

Some objections have been raised to AIH because of the method of collecting the semen. The simplest, though not the only, method is that of masturbation. The Anglican Committee set up by the Archbishop of Canterbury said: 'The act which produces the seminal fluid, being in this instance directed towards the completion (impossible without it) of the procreative end of the marriage, loses its character of self-abuse. It cannot in this view be the will of God that a husband and wife should remain childless merely because an act of this kind is required to promote conception.'[18] This judgement is

[17] General interest in this subject is recent, though there is evidence of experiments with animals and human beings over a long period of time. The first recorded instance of successful AIH is that of an operation performed in 1790 by an English physician, John Hunter, on the wife of a linen draper in the Strand.
[18] *Artificial Human Insemination* (London 1948), p. 58.

not upheld by the Roman Catholic Church, which condemns AIH because, in the words of Pope Pius XI, it 'violates the natural law'.[19]

AID has been generally condemned by those Churches which have pronounced upon it, though individual Christians have expressed their approval of it as a method of relieving the disability of childless couples. The Methodist Conference, in its 1958 Resolution, said:

'In the case of AID it is recognized that those who involve themselves in this practice, whether as recipients, donors, or physicians, may do so because of high motives. The Conference is sympathetically aware of the situation confronting many married people who are involuntarily childless. But the exclusive sexual union of man and wife is of the essence of marriage as the Christian understands the mind and purpose of God. To destroy that exclusiveness, therefore, is to thwart the purpose of God. Thus, adultery, which is wrong for several reasons, is wrong chiefly because it does so thwart the divine purpose. It is because the exclusive union between man and wife is also invaded by the giving and receiving of the seed of the donor that AID is wrong.'

At the heart of this pronouncement there is a theological judgement about the nature of marriage. It is claimed that the exclusiveness of the sexual relationship between man and wife is of the essence of marriage and that AID constitutes an invasion of that exclusiveness. That is to say, although it would be misleading to speak of AID as 'adultery', it would be factually correct to describe it as 'adulterous'. It was recognized during the discussions which led to the formulation of this judgement that it was not possible as yet to base any conclusion on the

---

[19] For a full discussion of the Roman Catholic and other attitudes to AIH, see *Life, Death, and the Law*, Norman St John-Stevas (Eyre & Spottiswoode, 1961), pp. 116-59.

SCIENTIFIC INVASION 133

evidence about the psychological and sociological consequences of AID. Such evidence is practically non-existent, though there is plenty of speculation about the effects of this practice on children so conceived, and on the attitudes of the partners in the marriage, and on the donor of the seed. The most exhaustive study of the subject so far undertaken in this country resulted from the appointment in September 1958 of a Government committee under the chairmanship of Lord Feversham with the following terms of reference:

'To enquire into the existing practice of artificial insemination and its legal consequences and to consider whether taking account of the interests of individuals involved and of society as a whole, any change in the law is necessary or desirable.'

The committee published its Report in July 1960.[20] Its main concern was with the legal position, though its discussions ranged widely. It concluded that AID should be neither prohibited nor regulated by law. But the committee added: 'The fact that we do not recommend restrictive legislation does not mean that we are indifferent to the practice or that we lack decision in our attitude to it. . . . We are clear in our opinion that having regard to the dangers and disadvantages for the child, the parents, and the donor, and for society as a whole, AID is undesirable. We therefore wish to discourage the practice.'[21]

(d) Other techniques which are the subjects of experiments with animals

Before artificial human insemination became a matter of public concern the technique of AI had, of course, been

[20] *Report of the Departmental Committee on Human Artificial Insemination*, Cmd. 1105 (H.M.S.O.).
[21] Ibid. p. 79.

perfected and widely adopted in the realm of animal husbandry. The Milk Marketing Board report that in 1944 they had one centre for this purpose and that 2,599 cows were inseminated. By 1949 they had 22 centres and the number of cows inseminated had risen to 431,370. In 1958, with the same number of centres, the number of cows was 1,449,765. These figures indicate the phenomenal rate of development. In 1958 nearly two-thirds of the national dairy herd were inseminated through the work of these and other centres. Calves conceived by natural, as distinct from artificial process, now form a decreasing minority. The same technique is developing in relation to sheep and pigs.

These facts are interesting, indeed fascinating in themselves, but the point in referring to them here is to indicate the way in which a technique, perfected in the realm of animal husbandry, can be applied to human beings. This raises the question whether there may not be an imminent prospect of a 'break-through' of a similar kind in respect of other techniques which are the subject of experiments with animals. There can be no doubt about the answer to this question. Animal sperms can be stored in deep freeze for long periods; fertilized ova can be similarly stored and transplanted; experiments are being carried out in methods of inducing multiple births; sex selection has been attempted with a measure of success. These cryptic notes provide us with a glimpse into a highly-specialized field where much is happening with remarkable speed. Opinions vary as to the extent to which some of these techniques may become applicable to human beings, but it may, in some cases, be sooner than we imagine. The strange world of George Orwell's '1984' seems to be not so far away after all.

To take just one of the items referred to: let us suppose

that before long parents have it within their power to decide the sex of the child to be conceived. The possibilities inherent in such a revolutionary change are far-reaching. Nature has shown a remarkable constancy in maintaining a rough, though slightly unequal balance, between the numbers of men and women in the world. If parents were free to choose the sex of their offspring would this materially alter the balance, or is the likelihood rather that the situation would look after itself? What controls, if any, would be needed, or should the use of the technique be banned? So, contemplation of the prospect leads from one difficult question to another, and also to the realization that judgements valid in one part of the world might be misleading in another (say, where the present outlook is strongly disposed to the glad acceptance of male off-spring and to disappointment when a girl is born).

A FUNDAMENTAL QUESTION

Behind all other questions about specific techniques directed to the achievement of certain ends there looms up the larger and quite fundamental question: How far is Man justified in using the powers which enable him to act decisively in spheres which were once regarded as reserved for God's sole action? When we are talking of the use of scientific means to combat sickness, hunger, famine and ignorance the answer is clear enough. We are in no doubt that God has called us to be co-workers with Him, and that it is His will that we should continue to uncover the secrets of power locked up in His universe. The eager desire for knowledge is something that our Creator has planted within us. It is within the purpose of Providence that we should advance in knowledge, just as it is part of God's plan that we should grow towards that spiritual and moral maturity which will enable us rightly to use the new powers which discovery releases. Professor C. A. Coulson has warned us against believing in a 'God of the gaps'. It is disastrous to think of God as one who operates only in those areas where as yet man is powerless to help himself, for then, as we close the gaps, we push God out of our lives, instead of enthroning Him at the centre of all our activity and experience.

If we are agreed that we are called to be co-workers with God, and if it is comparatively easy to see what this means in terms of using our newly-won powers in the fight against disease and kindred evils, the right response is not so clear when we come to consider the use of those powers which are likely to be soon within our grasp affecting our fundamental responsibility of procreation. As we glance back over the second half of this chapter and note again the various judgements which the Churches have made about contraception and other means of family limitation, and about artificial human insemination, is it possible to discern any guiding principle at work, informing those pronouncements?

The answer to this most important question can be given in one sentence. Behind all the judgements of the Church on the matters referred to there is a respect for human personality. This respect is based squarely on the belief that men and women have been made for fellowship with God; their true destiny is to become real persons, fully human. This achievement of personality is made possible only through right relationship—with other persons and supremely with the One Person who, to echo the great words of Augustine, has made us for Himself so that our hearts are restless until they find their rest in Him.

It is because the creation of a person depends upon relationship with others that God made sex. Out of the creative meeting of two persons comes the environment into which a child may be born. It is because the child is born into a relationship that it is possible for it to become a person. There is no such thing as a person living for and by himself.

This may seem to be labouring the obvious, but it is of paramount importance that the point should be fully grasped because of the practical corollary which follows. This is that all the proposals about the use of scientific techniques aimed at the control not only of the numbers but the kind of persons to be born shall be judged by the criterion as to whether they threaten or improve the prospect of a truly personal life.

This emphasis on the unique importance of personality and personal relationships is found repeatedly in the Bible, and particularly in the gospels. It lies at the heart of the method which Jesus chose in calling out a small band of men, and living with them for what most Churches would regard as an absurdly short ministry. During that period they were free to go if they wanted to, and one of them did. Christ would not force Judas, nor any man, because this would not be in keeping with his purpose for Man.

The application of this principle of respect for Man as a person—in relationship to the complex issues already raised by the invasion of science into the deepest realms of human experience—is no easy task. This much is clear as a result of discussions, and disagreements, about the techniques described in this chapter. It is likely to be even more difficult as more new powers become available to men. Though it may be a long time before some of the dreams of the more imaginative eugenists become capable of realization, events move so swiftly that we may expect many spectacular advances. To regard the pursuit of new knowledge as a devilish misuse of human faculties is to call in question the wisdom of God who created those faculties. It is from Him, too, that we derive the light whereby we may walk without stumbling, rightly sifting truth from falsehood, and discerning the details of His ever-expanding purposes. The world which the scientist explores is God's world. The results of the scientist's investigations demand a deeper doctrine of divine providence.

The unbiased reader may feel that this chapter supplies at least some evidence that, however reluctant the Churches may have been in the past to face up to the challenge of change, they are in these days not unaware of the need for forward-looking thinking. A further indication of this is to be seen in the setting up by the British Council of Churches of a Working Party with the following terms of reference:

'To give general consideration, in the light of the Christian faith, to emergent moral problems in connection with human conception and birth and, in particular, artificial insemination, the prevention of nidation, and other related matters.'

This Group began its work in 1959 and hopes to present a report of its findings later this year. It is doubtful whether any other group has tried to cover quite the same ground, and it is to be hoped that the results of its thinking will stimulate a wider discussion of the important issues which have been under consideration.

Our examination of the scientific invasion which is so greatly affecting the relationship of men and women, as of every other aspect of life, can fittingly conclude with another quotation from Sir John Russell: 'Once again science and religion are brought face to face. In the old days it was in conflict about dogma; now it is to co-operate in solving (these) serious and extremely complex problems of human relationships. Those young people of today, who will be the leaders of thought and of action tomorrow, are faced with the problem of ensuring that, in gaining control over Nature, man does not lose his own soul.[22]

[22] *Science and Modern Life*, p. 101.

CHAPTER SEVEN

INTERLUDE FOR THEOLOGY

SCATTERED over the preceding pages are a number of references to shifts in theological emphasis and interpretation, and to the need for restatement of the Christian view of the meaning and significance of human sexuality. We have examined some of the factors which have undermined parts of the Christian sexual tradition, and noted the kind of response to new situations which has come from within the Churches. Implicit in much of this has been the assumption that theology is not indifferent to the changing patterns of human life, but that indeed it is very much concerned with them, and has something vital to say to Man in his pilgrimage from a storied past to an unknown future. We shall now examine that assumption more closely, and take particular note of the importance of certain great Christian doctrines for a true understanding of Man, Woman, and their relationship. We are bound to refer again to some points which have already been made, but it will be useful to set them now in a framework of theological doctrine.

THE RELEVANCE OF THEOLOGY

According to the *Oxford English Dictionary* theology is 'The study of science which treats of God, His nature and attributes, and His relations with man and the universe'. Christian theology is, of course, theology as it has been understood and studied by Christians. Even with that limitation, it is a very considerable business; so much so that it seems almost ludicrous that we should devote one short chapter to the theological aspects of our subject.

However, it is worth trying to make a few important points a little clearer, and we may begin by spelling out more fully the dictionary definition of theology.

The first thing to be said about theology is that it could not exist at all but for two facts. One of these is that God exists, and the other is that He has revealed Himself to men, and continues to do so. These two facts constitute the basic presupposition which the science of theology exists to investigate. If it be objected that theology cannot be designated a science because science does not make presuppositions, the answer is that in fact science also makes presuppositions. As one well-known scientist has put it, science is based on two basic beliefs: 'One is the belief that nature is a coherent unity. . . . The other basic belief of science is that nature is accessible to the human mind.'[1]

Of course, theology is different from other sciences because it is also part of its presupposition that God is a person and not a thing; and this Person has made Himself known in personal dealings with men, most especially through one race of men—the Jews.

Now, although our concern has been with the impact of various modern developments on one limited aspect of the Christian tradition, it is, of course, true that the whole of theology has been facing a crisis. The theological presupposition to which we have just referred tended to be linked with the idea of the Bible as a kind of holy island in a secular sea, an inerrant book utterly divorced from all other literature. Men might believe, as John Robinson said to the Pilgrim Fathers, that 'The Lord hath more light and truth yet to break forth out of His Holy Word', but the Record remained immutable and exempt from the tampering minds of secular critics.

In a variety of ways this position has been undermined.

[1] *The Humanist Frame* (Allen & Unwin, 1961). Chapter 4, by J. Bronowski, p. 88.

The literary and historical criticism of the biblical text has shown that it has much in common with other literature, and so the rigid distinction between sacred and secular, natural and supernatural, has become untenable. Moreover, the searchlight of scientific enquiry has been thrown on to the pages of the Bible to reveal that it contains many misstatements and inconsistencies. A rigid belief in the inerrancy of Scripture can no longer be defended.

Faced with this situation some Christians have buried their heads in the sand. It is doubtful whether even the most rigid fundamentalist is entirely immune from the effects of modern scholarship, though some appear to have provided themselves with a remarkably effective insulation. At the other extreme there are those who seem to have opened their minds so wide to the winds of change that their Christian convictions have been blown away, to be replaced by a vague religiosity expressed in a jumble of ill-digested scientific jargon.

In between these two extremes there are, happily, a great many who occupy a mediating position. Many of the great names in modern theological study like Paul Tillich, Reinhold Niebuhr, Karl Barth and Emil Brunner would refuse to be identified with either extremist School, though extremist labels may be attached to them by those who do not share their views.

Dr Alec R. Vidler, the Dean of King's College, Cambridge, in an interesting essay on the future of theology, asks whether that future is likely to be with either of the extreme Schools or with the mediating theologians, or with none of them. His conclusion is both perceptive and suggestive. After noting that the ablest of the mediating theologians are to be found in the universities, he goes on to say: 'Academic theologians may carry conviction to their pupils and supply their needs. But few of them have so far shown a capacity for convincing laymen engaged in other disciplines and walks of life that theology has anything to say to them or to do with them. Yet theology, if its presupposition is valid, is a subject that must vitally concern everyone. No one in his senses will suppose that there is a God who has revealed himself only for the benefit of clergymen and teachers of divinity. . . . If theology is to have a future of any consequence, we may hazard the conjecture that it will have to cease to be an almost clerical monopoly. It will have to win the interest of laymen. It will have to command their intellectual respect and to capture their imagination and then give them free scope to play their part in theological thinking. Books by theologians that succeed in showing that theology has to do with the profoundest and most baffling of contemporary issues . . . ring bells for laymen who are quite untouched by conventional clerical theologizing.'[2]

Dr Vidler's prophetic words should fortify us as we look at three basic Christian doctrines, the discussion of which must contribute powerfully to any attempt at fresh understanding of God's purpose in making us men and women. They are the doctrines of creation, of sin, and of salvation. We shall remember that we are not dealing with a fixed and unalterable tradition because we are not dealing with a God who can be imprisoned in the strait-jacket of any human formulation. Theological fossils are instructive, and what they tell us is not by any means irrelevant to our present needs. But it must always be remembered that the life which once dwelt within them has evolved into more complex forms, shaped by the spiritual life-force within, adapting itself to pressures from without.

THE DOCTRINE OF CREATION

The Bible begins with the story of creation. Its opening phrase is 'In the beginning God created'. It is true that

[2] *Essays in Liberality* (SCM, 1957), pp. 37-9.

the Book of Genesis is not the first in chronological sequence of the books of the Bible, but the fact of the divine creation is the only point at which the Bible could begin. Emil Brunner stresses the fundamental nature of the fact with which the Bible opens: 'The first word of the Bible is the word Creator and creation. But that is not simply the first word with which one begins in order to pass on to greater, more important matters. It is the primeval word supporting everything else. Take it away and everything collapses. Indeed if one rightly understands that which the Bible means by the Creator, one has rightly understood the whole Bible.'[3]

We have already noted (in Chapter 1) the naturalistic outlook of the Hebrew people which was a reflection of their acceptance of the belief that God had made all things out of nothing, and that 'God saw everything that He had made, and, behold, it was very good' (Gen 1[12].) We also observed the disastrous results of the distortion of this doctrine by the influence of Greek thought and Oriental dualism. This led to a dichotomy between spiritual and material, soul and flesh, and the consequent spread of an otherworldliness which eschewed earthly pleasures, and produced a morbid antipathy to the human body, and its sexual functions in particular.

The full recovery of the profound significance of the doctrine of divine creation is of paramount importance if we are to recognize sex as something good in itself. Like all the other gifts of God it can, very obviously, be abused, and, because of the fact of man's sin (which we shall consider later), it often is. But if sex is a gift of God, and not a devilish device to entice men and women, and then to ensnare them in misery, it is all-important to discover the mind and purpose of the Creator concerning it.

One of the unfortunate results of Christians taking up

[3] *Our Faith* (SCM, 1936), p. 24.

INTERLUDE FOR THEOLOGY 145

wrong and indefensible positions is to be seen in the fact that many who have zealously contended for the literal accuracy of the Genesis accounts of creation have failed to observe the far-reaching significance of what the story has to tell us about sex. In the account of the creation of Man contained in Genesis 1 we are told: 'And God created man in his own image, in the image of God created he him; male and female created he them' (verse 27). In the preceding verse God says: 'Let us make man in our image, after our likeness.'

Various explanations have been advanced of the conception of the divine image in the mind of the writer of the first chapter of Genesis. Patristic exegesis emphasized Man's rationality and freedom as the central constituents of his likeness to God. Some have suggested that the use of the plural forms 'us' and 'our' indicate an original polytheistic belief about deity; others have maintained that they are merely the plurals of majesty. Tertullian believed that the writer of Genesis 1 held something approaching our Trinitarian doctrine.

The fact is that we cannot know precisely what was in the mind of the writer. What we do know, because we have been given a fuller revelation of God's nature, is that He is a social Being. The doctrine of the Trinity 'is the affirmation of a full rich life in God as distinct from all abstract and barren conceptions of his being'.[4] We know God as a unity of three Persons. Whether or not this was in any sense clear to the writer of Genesis 1, we may take his essential point that God made Man in His own image, adding to the assertion our own knowledge of the fact that God is a 'Being in relation'.

In making man, then, God has stamped him with this special mark which distinguishes him from all other

[4] *Outline of Christian Theology*, W. Adams Brown (T. & T. Clark, 1910), p. 162.

creatures: he becomes a person by entering into relationship with others. Take a baby and set it down in a tribe of monkeys and it will grow up as an animal. It will have the potential of personality, but that potential will remain undeveloped. A monkey transferred from its native habitat to a travelling circus may become a family favourite, but never a member of the family. The importance of man as a person was the point which guided our thinking when, near the end of the previous chapter, we were considering the principle which should guide us in the use of techniques affecting conception and birth. Martin Buber, the great Jewish philosopher, has summed up this important truth in a sentence: 'As a Person God gives personal life, he makes us as persons become capable of meeting with him and with one another.'[5] Paul Tillich, emphasizing the immense influence which Buber has had on Protestant theological thought, sums up much of the message of the small but potent volume *I and Thou* in these words: 'There is no other way of becoming an "I" than by meeting a "Thou" and by accepting it as such, and there is no other way of meeting and accepting a "Thou" than by meeting and accepting the "Eternal Thou" in the finite "Thou".'[6]

We turn again to the work of Dr D. Sherwin Bailey for some further comments on the significance of the biblical account of Man as created in God's image. He points out that there is a conflict between the views of Barth and Brunner as to the precise nature of that which constitutes the image of God in Man. 'Barth maintains . . . that the relational image of God in its Manward aspect is specifically and exclusively sexual, and consists in the general relationship of man and woman. Brunner, on the other hand, finds the image in every responsible I-Thou relation, and criticizes Barth's view on the ground that

[5] *I and Thou*, 2nd British Edition (T. & T. Clark, 1958), p. 136.
[6] *Theology of Culture* (OUP, 1959), p. 189.

sexual polarity is not itself "the distinctive element in Man which differentiates him from all other creatures", but is only "one strand in this element".'[7] Dr Bailey accepts Brunner's conception of the image but maintains that it fails to take fully into account the inner meaning of sexual polarity. 'Sex in Man is more than a mere faculty or attribute—much more, certainly, than a generative or venereal phenomenon. In the race, it is a divisive factor separating humanity into two radically different yet mutually complementary elements—male and female; in the individual, it is an informing and governing principle which permeates his being to its depths, and conditions every facet of his personality and his life.'[8] The conclusion is 'that Man is a "two-fold" being, not simply in respect of the neighbour relation, but also and pre-eminently in respect of the sexual relation; and that the latter is of such a kind and quality as to constitute in a special and peculiar sense the Manward relational aspect of the *imago Dei*'.[9]

The value of this approach to the metaphysical meaning of sexuality is that it not only expands the connotation of the word itself and releases it from bondage to that which is merely physical, but indicates the centrality of sex in the creative purpose of God. The fact that God made Man in two halves was not merely that by the union of man and woman the race might be continued, but also that by their fellowship they might experience that wholeness which is His will for Man.

The account of the creation of the first Man and Woman given in the second chapter of Genesis is different from that in the first chapter.[10] In the second chapter

[7] *The Man-Woman Relationship in Christian Thought*, p. 268.
[8] Ibid. p. 269.   [9] Ibid. p. 270.
[10] The account in Chapter 1 is the later of the two and is taken from the 'priestly' source of the Pentateuch, known as 'P'; the account in Chapter 2 is taken from the 'Yahwist' source known as 'J'.

there is no reference to the image of God, and instead of a simultaneous creation of the Man and the Woman, the Woman is made out of a rib taken from the Man's side while he slept. It is unfortunate that this myth has been wrongly used to give a spurious foundation to the androcentric tradition of the Christian Church. In spite of the differences between the two narratives, however, the relational principle is stated in the earlier of the two in the words which our Lord Himself quoted: 'Therefore shall a man leave his father and his mother, and shall cleave unto his wife: and they shall be one flesh.'[11]

The exposition of the meaning of sex, as rooted in the purpose of God to make persons capable of entering into relationship with one another and with Himself, leaves us in no doubt that there is no possibility of our escaping the fact of our sex even if we wanted to. The whole negative fear of sex, and the attempts to run away from it, reflected in the struggles of men and women down the ages, are seen not only as a mistake, but a tragedy. A man might as well try to jump out of his skin as leave his sex behind. It colours every thought he thinks and determines every action he performs, for always he must think and act as a man. Similarly a woman must always think and act as a woman.

If this sounds like labouring the obvious, it must be said that the phrases we have just used are not as simple or as straightforward as they sound. We have already noted the various social roles which in differing cultures have been allocated to men and women. There is no universal agreement as to what things are manly and womanly. How then can we find out the inner meanings of maleness and femaleness? Or is there no real answer to the question?

It may seem strange to pose these questions in an age

[11] Genesis 2^{24} (cited Matthew 19^5 and Mark 10^7).

INTERLUDE FOR THEOLOGY 149

which talks so much about sex and often with the confidence that it knows all the answers. It will be a salutory discipline if we can bring ourselves to recognize that we know very little, but that we are being given the chance to learn much more. For our line of thought leads to the conclusion that the deepest meanings of maleness and femaleness are not discovered by reading books, though such reading may help us to see how discovery may be made. The teaching of Buber is again suggestive and throws light on the way in which the Bible refers to sexual relationship as 'knowing'. 'And Adam knew his wife' (Gen 4^{25}). 'And Joseph . . . took unto him his wife; and knew her not till she had brought forth a son' (Mt 1^{24-5}, *RV*). The use of the word 'knew' is not a polite euphemism for 'had intercourse with her' (*NEB*): the Bible shows no reluctance to call a spade a spade. The word implies that Man cannot know the meaning of manhood without Woman; neither can Woman know the meaning of womanhood without Man.

The principle just stated has an obvious significance in marriage, for marriage is essentially the intimate encounter of a man and a woman. But it also has a wider application. Men and women have to live together, whether they are married or not. The secret of right relationship can only be revealed in the actual business of entering into responsible partnership and into fellowship based on mutual respect. The erosion of the old idea that this is a 'man's world' makes possible a new depth of understanding of the meaning of sex and the purposes of God in creating Man male and female. The truth about the world which God created is that it is not a man's world at all. It is Man's world, and Man, in the sense of mankind, is male and female. The society God wills for His children is a mutual society.

It is necessary before proceeding farther to look once

again at the Pauline doctrine of male headship. We have earlier dismissed it as a reflection of the kind of male arrogance which has accepted unquestioningly the *status quo*, and used the Genesis narrative to provide a theological justification for the subordination of women. We must not overlook, however, the arguments of such distinguished theologians as Dr E. L. Mascall, who contends that, even though the Genesis story of creation is a myth, this does not mean that it contains no theological truth. And further, though the story reflects a social fact of the time—namely, the subordination of women—the writer, like St Paul later, believed this to be in accordance with God's will. If we accept the authority of the Bible we cannot overlook the fact that much of its truth is the result of prophetic insight into historical situations and contemporary events.

Some writers, especially those who are strongly opposed to the idea of women in the ministry, have appealed to the fact that our Saviour was a man as evidence that it is the male sex which constitutes the true human nature made in God's image. It is not enough to say that the maleness of Jesus is just part of the 'scandal of particularity'; so was His Jewish nationality, but it was no mere accident that He was born into the Hebrew race. This latter point is one that we have ourselves argued in affirming that theologically it is the Jewish rather than the Greek tradition which was affirmed by the Incarnation as the Truth to which we must conform.

It is consistent with this point of view to believe that when Paul referred to the headship of the male he was not merely approving the popular idea of the superiority of the man, nor, in citing the Genesis story was he trying to invest the notion with scriptural authority. He was actually enunciating the doctrine that Woman derives her being from Man. The Greek word κεφαλή (head) is closely associated with the word ἀρχή (beginning). If this view is to be taken seriously it must be understood in some sense other than the purely biological. Biologically it is equally true to say that man is 'born of a woman'. It must be assumed that what is really meant is that Woman derives from Man her existence in the image of God. Woman does not exist in the image of God in herself and by herself, whereas Man does. The practical corollary of this is that Woman can only hear and obey God by hearing and obeying Man.

This theological interpretation is obviously opposed to the one which we have previously elaborated. Although accepted by some with great sincerity, it results from too rigid an exegis of one section of the Genesis narrative and some of the Pauline deductions from it. Moreover, it is theological reasoning too much divorced from the actualities of human experience. It is difficult to make sense of it in the context of the living fellowship of the modern Church to which women are making so notable a contribution. Is it perhaps too much to hope that when we get a few more women theologians this unfortunate doctrine may finally be laid to rest?

THE DOCTRINE OF SIN

The biblical account of creation is followed immediately by the story of the Fall. We mentioned earlier (p. 7) that it is a mistake to suppose that the first sin of Adam and Eve was sexual. Their sin was that of pride, of self-centredness, the desire to usurp the place of God. Because Man is free to respond to God and fulfil his destiny, he is also free to reject God and accomplish his own downfall. The image of God in Man becomes blurred as the creature spurns his Creator, and the result of this is the element of estrangement and division which enters into every kind of relationship. This is the significance of those vivid verses which tell how the first Man and his wife made aprons of fig leaves and tried to hide from God among the trees in the Garden (Gen 3[7-8]).

It is a fact of great significance that the immediate result of sin was that Adam and Eve became anxious and suspicious: their confidence and trust were shattered. Reinhold Niebuhr discusses in his Gifford Lectures this sense of anxiety which is the fruit of sin. He speaks of Man as a free and responsible being, but it is that very responsible freedom which gives rise to anxiety. There are only two ways of escape from this anxiety. A man can trust God and enter into a creative relationship with Him and with his fellows; or he can attempt to find security in the only thing he is sure of, which is himself. The latter way, of course, is not an avenue of escape at all, but a road of disillusionment.

The ubiquity of anxiety is a familiar theme in the writings of psychoanalysts. Different writers use different terms, but they all emphasize the same point. Some, like Jung, refer to man's need for a sense of security; others, like Adler, refer to the necessity of a sense of significance; and the case histories quoted provide a tragic wealth of human evidence in support of the contention that anxiety is the seed-bed of neurosis.

There is a good deal of common ground here between theologians and psychologists. Both are agreed about the universal presence of this anxiety which can be disruptive of happiness and even of life itself. (Behind many cases of suicide there is a feeling of being unloved and of no significance, and a consequent lack of any sense of security). There is also agreement that behaviour is symptomatic. That is to say, it is no good trying to deal with the symptoms, which are the overt actions of men and women, unless you penetrate to their inner meaning and motivation.

INTERLUDE FOR THEOLOGY 153

This emphasis on the importance of motivation is to be seen clearly in all Our Lord's dealings with men and women. In the Sermon on the Mount He says: 'You have learned that they were told, "Do not commit adultery." But what I tell you is this: If a man looks on a woman with a lustful eye, he has already committed adultery with her in his heart' (Mt 5^{27-8}). Again, after a dispute with the Pharisees about the ceremonial washing of hands, Jesus says in answer to a question from his rather dull-witted disciples: 'Do you not see that whatever goes in by the mouth passes into the stomach and so is discharged into the drain? But what comes out of the mouth has its origins in the heart; and that is what defiles a man. Wicked thoughts, murder, adultery, fornication, theft, perjury, slander—these all proceed from the heart; and these are the things that defile a man' (Mt 15^{17-20}).

It was evident when we were discussing the question of the moral atmosphere of our times (in Chapter 4) that the attempt to explain anti-social behaviour rather than merely to say 'It is Sin' makes it difficult to hold rigidly to some of the traditional categories of Christian thought. The tendency to equate sin with sickness is often deplored by Christian moralists, and indeed it has its perils. But there is a very real sense in which we are taken nearer to the New Testament by the insistence on the necessity to probe the motives of delinquency and discover why men and women behave as they do. What very often hinders us in our acceptance of this suggestion is that we are more concerned to condemn than to save; we cannot escape from the fateful desire to sit in judgement on our neighbour. Consequently, because we are little people, our estimate of the situation is narrow and moralistic, and our solution is as pathetically inadequate as our diagnosis.

Only when we have grasped the fact that we are sinners

in no position to condemn any man, and redeemed only by the grace of God, are we able or fitted to bring to those who need it the word which saves and the insight which heals. We only realize the full extent of Man's need when we recognize the all-pervasiveness of sin. Every one of us suffers because of our own sin. It is equally true that we all suffer because of the sin of others. It is not part of our responsibility as Christians who desire the salvation of all men to apportion blame; when we try to do so we are bound to fail for we have no scales of justice capable of so complex a measurement. The word of Christ to us is 'Pass no judgement, and you will not be judged' (Mt 7[1]).

What has just been written is of special importance when we consider sexual delinquency. We have already referred (pp. 13–14) to the incident recorded in John 8 in which Jesus said to the woman detected in adultery: 'No more do I [condemn you]. You may go; do not sin again.' Here there is no attempt to camouflage sin. For Jesus, sin was primarily not what a man does, but what he is. The outward penalties of sin which we call upon ourselves are real enough; but far worse is the inner result of loss of fellowship with God. From this flow all the disruptive results of sin which are everywhere apparent.

This exposition of the meaning of sin and our approach to it does not leave out the reality of judgement. It does remind us that it is 'God [who] judges the secrets of human hearts' (Rom 2[16]). Neither does our exposition obscure the reality of God's law. He has made the world and His law runs through the whole law of life. Moreover, He has shown us that the whole law is summed up in the two-fold rule of love to God and our neighbour. We must always set before ourselves and others that the breaking of this law brings its own penalties and that the only satisfactory basis for living is conformity with that law. But

INTERLUDE FOR THEOLOGY 155

God's law is but an aspect of His love. To break the law of God is to turn away from love. God showed us the seriousness of this by dying on the Cross. In so doing He also revealed that the only remedy for sin is forgiveness, the restoration of the lost relationship.

The Christian approach to the problem of sexual deviation is to help the person to understand the true nature of his condition which is one of estrangement and poverty of full personal relationship. Condemnation will not help and moral exhortation will only increase despair. The only real answer to this problem is the experience of fellowship with God and mature and responsible relationship with others: the two aspects of what Christians call 'life in Christ'.

Some of the points which have been stated very briefly and inadequately in this section are expounded at length in Frederic Greeves's penetrating study of the meaning of Sin.[12] He criticizes the inadequate conceptions of sin which limit it to those thoughts and actions which consciously and deliberately break the law of God. He reveals the intense seriousness and far-reaching significance of what, when it is properly understood, is described by Charles Wesley as 'the depth of inbred sin'. We must accept the fact that our ignorance of ourselves is part of our sin, and the type of self-evaluation which sets out to produce a kind of personal balance sheet of moral assets and liabilities is itself an indication of our failure to recognize this. We must believe in the power of God to deal with the whole of our personality right down to its hidden depths.

Principal Greeves points out that, in view of our ignorance of ourselves, we must beware of expecting from others a self-knowledge which *we* know we cannot possess. We must 'recognize the limitations to our *moral* judgements

[12] *The Meaning of Sin* (Epworth Press, 1956).

upon other people. Even the moral evaluation of particular actions is a precarious task, but when judgement concerns character, the fallibility of man's moral assessment of his fellows becomes obvious, to all but those who are either self-righteous or superficial in their thinking'.[13]

Some further comments by the same author lead us into a final section on the importance for the proper understanding of the problems of sex of the Christian doctrine of salvation.

THE DOCTRINE OF SALVATION

Principal Greeves writes about the difficulties and dangers of denunciation. 'That there is a place for such denunciation cannot be denied, although Christians, with monotonous consistency, are prone to denounce the type of offenders, and the kind of offence, which our Lord treated with gentleness, and to deal lightly with those that incurred His wrath. It must never be forgotten, however, that if denunciation could have sufficed there would have been no occasion for the death of Christ.'[14]

'When sin is interpreted in purely moralistic terms, it is easy for us to lose sight of the fact that to tell men about their sinfulness is to bring them good news. That would not, of course, be true were it not for the proclamation of God's forgiveness, of His victory over sin; nevertheless, we need to regain the conviction that it is *good* for men to learn the truth about their predicament, so that they may no longer walk in darkness.'[15]

The importance of a therapeutic rather than a censorious attitude to the sexual problems and irregularities of men and women should by now be fairly obvious. It is all to the good that in the new emphasis on counselling in the training of the Christian ministry we are recovering

[13] *The Meaning of Sin*, p. 169.   [14] Ibid. p. 170.   [15] Ibid. p. 171.

INTERLUDE FOR THEOLOGY 157

something of the rich significance of such terms as 'the pastoral office' and 'the cure of souls'.

If sin is essentially estrangement and its result anxiety arising from lack of the security of right relationship, the key word in the understanding of salvation is reconciliation. The theological word 'atonement' is the theme of the biblical account of God's redemptive purposes. The Bible speaks not of one Adam but of two. Jesus was the second Adam who 'to the fight and to the rescue came'. The story of Jesus begins with the fact of incarnation. He came 'widest extremes to join'. His characteristic method of teaching was the use of the parable: an earthly story with a heavenly meaning. When he healed the sick He revealed His understanding of the psychosomatic nature of personality by using the formula: 'Be thou made whole.' Before His death He sat at a table with His disciples and made material elements the vehicle of spiritual grace, so setting at the heart of the Church's liturgy conjointly the work of God and the work of Man. (Incidentally, it is not without meaning for our subject that one of the great movements making for renewal in the life of the modern Church is the revival of interest in liturgy and particularly the Holy Communion. Inseparable from this is a deeper appreciation of the significance of the material.) When the Saviour died it was on a cross erected outside the city wall, for the temple veil was torn in two, and the division between sacred and secular healed. And there were signs in the heavens, as there had been at His birth, for

> *Nature and grace, with all their powers*
> *Confess the infinite unknown.*

The key word in all this activity of redeeming love is reconciliation, the healing of division, the restoration of relationship.

True Christianity, like psychoanalysis, is anti-moralistic. It is concerned with the transformation of the whole personality rather than the suppression of symptoms. There is need to encourage all those attempts which happily are now being made to bring together psychiatrists and pastors, and indeed, physicians, too. Co-operation can achieve a cure of conditions which have defied the attempts which have failed to recognize that men and women are essentially a unity of body, mind, and soul.

There is only one thing that can cast out the fear and anxiety which so often lie behind anti-social conduct, and that is love. The Christian doctrine of salvation witnesses to the fact that men and women can undergo a transformation and reorientation of attitude. They can indeed be 'born again' (significant phrase) into a world of new relationships. This happens when they face and accept the ultimate fact about who they are and what is wrong with them. When we accept the fact that we belong to God we accept as axiomatic that we belong to one another. It is on this basis of personal and social realization that we are able to enter into mature and responsible relationship, leaving behind the need for all those reparative activities which reflect our inner anxiety and lack of security.

So it is that a man can only find his life in losing it. For we have no life of our own: life is in relationship. There is no individual salvation, only personal, and therefore, social. Hence the invitation of Christ is to enter a Kingdom. The way to that Kingdom is impeded both by negative renunciation of that sexuality, which is a means of relationship, and by theories of inequality which misinterpret God's plan. The resolute rejection of both these errors is essential if we are to affirm the positive meaning of redemption and seek

> [*That*] *domain,*
> *In which all lesser hopes*
> *Are crowned*
> *At last.*[16]

[16] *Who Made Me a Divider?* R. J. Barker (Meridian Books, 1949), p. 223.

CHAPTER EIGHT

PROGRESS IN PARTNERSHIP

IT IS PART of the discipline of life that we should always be asking questions to which at the moment there seems to be no adequate answer. This fact should never deter us in our quest for truth. If we cannot find all the answers, at least let us try to discover the right questions. It will avail us little in our understanding of life and our capacity to live well if we find the answer to the wrong question.

In our present study we have raised a great many questions. In some cases it has been possible to suggest the outline of a constructive answer; but often it has been apparent that the solution of a problem awaits a fuller realization of co-operation which is the key to so many of life's mysteries. What Jesus said about knowledge of God is particularly true of the problems of sexual relationship: they who do shall know. It is by entering into responsible personal fellowship that men and women discover the meaning of manhood and womanhood, and how the one complements and fulfils the other. This is the conclusion to which we have come.

As we look back over the journey we have made there is one fact which stands out beyond all the others: it is the fact of change. It is not merely the fact of change but its bewildering rapidity which impresses us. Long-established customs and old ways of thinking have been thrown so suddenly into the melting-pot. This twentieth century is a crucible out of which continue to pour a welter of new ideas: challenging old concepts, modifying old manners, and dissolving old disciplines. Through the haze of their own thoughts men peer to see if they can discern the shape of things to come.

In the introduction to this lecture, and before we plunged into the detailed discussion of our complicated theme, we reminded ourselves that the Christian's place was down in the arena of conflict, and not among the timid spectators, fearful of any real involvement in revolution. We return to this now at the end as the basis for several suggestions about the shape of our practical Christian responsibility.

THE FACT OF CHANGE

A few weeks before these words were written the death was announced at the age of 89 of Lord Pethick-Lawrence. The life of this remarkable man spanned a period of unprecedented revolution. He witnessed the birth of radio and television, the coming of the aeroplane, and the first steps in the conquest of space. The creation of the Welfare State at home and the repercussions of the Communist revolution abroad are part of the story of those crowded years. His career as a statesman reached its zenith when he led the historic cabinet mission to India in 1946, and shared in the onerous task of clearing the road to independence for that great country.

This brief reference to a distinguished statesman may serve to focus afresh in our minds both the fact and the rapidity of social change during the last century. It also reminds us of its complexity. The name of Pethick-Lawrence is linked inseparately with the battle for women's suffrage which, as we have seen, was but one aspect of the transformation of sexual relationship which has resulted from and contributed to the great changes which have affected every aspect of our life.

We cannot too often remind ourselves that Christianity was, in the mind of our Lord, a revolutionary religion.

He came not to bring peace but a sword. The message of the Kingdom is like leaven in the dough. It is like new wine, producing ferment. None of these sayings is to be taken literally, but all of them is to be received seriously. Repeatedly, like a sharp scythe cutting away the tangled undergrowth of outmoded tradition, Jesus says, 'You have heard that it used to be said. But I say . . .'

We ought, then, to be at home in a day of revolution. It is not that we welcome change for its own sake, nor that we suppose all change to be good. Rather it is that we expect change, see it as one of the evidences of God's activity, and seek always to guide it to His ends.

THE RELEVANCE OF CO-OPERATION

It is a fact to be noticed that very many of the achievements of the modern world are the result of co-operation. The major recent advances in atomic physics, according to one expert, are the result not of the labours of the individual research worker but of groups working in co-operation.

In industry, in spite of the tradition that the interests of employer and employees are opposed, the more enlightened among management and men see the need for and the value of a greater measure of partnership.

In agriculture the farmer is more and more dependent on the use of machinery, and so the rural and urban aspects of our society are forced together.

These, and many similar examples which might be cited, have relevance for the preaching of the gospel. It is increasingly recognized in the colleges where ministers are trained that we cannot as Christians escape the complex interplay of forces in modern life. Biblical and theological study must be informed by sociology and by some knowledge of the approach of science to reality. Only by such cross-fertilization will our traditional disciplines be made fruitful.

In one important aspect the co-operation which once characterized the family has left it. The industrialization of our society meant the break-up of the family as a working unit, earning its livelihood together. But happily, as we have seen, we are moving towards new sorts of co-operation and mutual sharing in the life of the home. One all-important element in that co-operation is the partnership of men and women who regard marriage as a democracy and not as a patriarchy.

What, then, in this rapidly-changing situation are the practical things which the Church must do? They may be briefly summarized by the four words: thinking, training, healing, and living.

THE TASK OF THE CHURCH

(a) Thinking

The Church must provide a 'service of thinking'. There are searching questions to be asked, but Christian people are not being sufficiently encouraged to ask them. Far too much valuable time is spent in unrelated Bible study and religious discussion which is vague rather than specific. Preachers should be helped to deal with the theological aspects of sexual relationship as part of the proclamation of the good news of the gospel. The rather superficial contention that 'the pulpit is not the place for sex education' is sometimes used as an excuse for the avoidance of a pressing duty. Of course the pulpit is not the place for a lecture on the biology of reproduction, but it is surely indefensible that preachers should remain silent about one of the quite inescapable facts of life. Our creation, our preservation, and all the blessings of this life are but different aspects of the loving providence of God. We must talk about them all.

There is special need for the clear presentation of the

Christian case for keeping coition within marriage. It is not sufficient to set this forth as a dogma that does not permit of reasoned argument. We must show that it is rooted in wisdom and insight into truth.

Because traditions vary in the Churches and in different parts of the world, the contribution of ecumenical discussion to this 'service of thinking' is of special importance. The growing recognition of the value of the work being done by the WCC Department on the Co-operation of Men and Women in Church and Society, and of smaller national groups working in the same field, is an encouraging sign. In Britain the decision to hold Home and Community Weeks throughout the country, beginning in the autumn of this year, results from an awareness among the Churches of the need for further exploration of the great questions we have been discussing. The younger Churches are feeling their way towards a greater uniformity of attitude towards polygamous marriages. We in this country should accept every invitation to share with them in their thinking.

(b) Training

The responsibility of the Churches for sex education is now widely recognized, though there is much uncertainty, and even some disagreement, as to how it ought to be done. There is a general agreement that it is not enough to impart biological information, and that, indeed, this can be so presented as to invoke the wrong kind of response from young people. Attitudes are all-important. Only by conveying the relational significance of sex can we hope to inculcate that respect for other people as persons which is the foundation of all right behaviour and satisfying friendship.

There is need for a great deal more discussion of how this can be done. It is partly a matter of the character and personality of the teaching. Right attitudes are communicable—and so, unfortunately, are wrong ones. But there is much to be learned from those who have achieved success in talking to young people.

Not the least valuable aspect of the right sort of discussion about sex is that it helps to provide those who take part in it with an adequate vocabulary. So many are tongue-tied simply because they are not sure of the right words to use. Because they are unfamiliar with the terms, they are afraid of looking foolish if they use the wrong word or mispronounce the right one. The teacher who can impart a proper vocabulary is doing more than increase the number of words which his hearers can use. The words we speak are a reflection of the thoughts we think, and the possession of an adequate vocabulary can be a means of mental emancipation.

It is also true that the Church's responsibility in preparing people for marriage is being taken more seriously. There is still much to be done before we are entirely rid of the scandal of the Church wedding which solemnly unites two people who are so ignorant that it will be a miracle if the marriage survives. Quite apart from it being our plain duty to see that those who are married in church are adequately prepared, it is an evangelistic opportunity. Only a deficient theology prevents our seeing this more clearly.

It is fundamental to any well-planned programme of education for marriage that an attempt should be made to help men and women to understand themselves and the complementary nature of their relationship.

(c) Healing

The co-operation between physicians, psychiatrists and pastors is making possible the healing of conditions which have defied a less unified approach to illness. Because man is a psychosomatic unity the roots of his sickness often go down deeply into body, mind, and soul. Consequently any adequate therapy must deal with all three.

In a similar way it is recognized that the healing of marriage, and the approach to problems of sexual relationship generally, necessitate the co-operation between different agencies whose specialized knowledge is needed if adequate solutions are to be found. The efficacy of the pastor's work is greatly increased if he is able to recognize the point at which he must turn a needy person over to the expert—and also if he knows where the expert is to be found. It is very important that there should be the right kind of co-operation between the marriage guidance and the family planning movements, because they have much to offer to each other.

One of the good results of co-operation is that insights gained in one field are seen to have significance in another. Perhaps the most important result of partnership between psychiatrists and pastors is that the latter have seen the necessity of a positive and redemptive approach to the problems of sexual maladjustment, and the dangers of a moralistic and 'holier than thou' attitude.

(d) Living

When all else has been said, the supreme requirement is that the Church should live out its message and be the embodiment of the kind of fellowship in which men and women learn the true meaning of partnership. The opportunities confronting Christ's people are many and varied; some of them are almost frightening in their challenge. Many of them we have glimpsed in the course of our study, and our consideration of them has raised questions which demand an answer. How can we move our Churches away from concentration on single-sex activities and towards that mutual fellowship in which men and women learn with and from each other? Can theological objections to the ordination of women to the Christian ministry stand against the moving and convincing testimony of some who have heard the call of God and been so ordained? How can we use our deeper and wider understanding of the meaning of sexuality to help the single man or woman—some of whom remain celibate by choice—to enter into deep and satisfying relationships? This last is a question we can only raise. Its importance is clear enough in an age when so often the single person, by reason of economic independence, is no longer an integral part of a closely-knit family structure.

So they continue to pour in upon the mind: the questions that must be asked. And if many of them are new and unfamiliar questions, let us not be discouraged. The fact that we are asking them is a sign of progress. The growing realization that we can only find the answers as men and women seek them together is a sign of progress in partnership. It is an earnest of that mutual society which God wills for His children, whom from the beginning He created male and female, after His own image, that they might learn from each other the meaning of the life which He bestows.

INDEX

Abraham, 8
Acepsurias, 28
Adler, 152
Affluence, 88
Africa, 95
Allen, Dr Clifford, 122
Amazone, 9
Animal husbandry, new techniques, 134
Anxiety, 152
Apphia, 20
Aquinas, 38, 40, 41, 128
Aristides, 26
Aristophanes, 9
Aristotle, 9, 39, 123
Artificial human insemination, 88, 131-5
Augustine, Confessions of, 32-7, 39, 41, 120
Australia, 52

Bailey, Dr D. Sherwin, 2, 109, 119, 146, 147
Baldwin, Stanley, 44
Barker, R. J., 159
Barth, Karl, 142
Basil, St, 28
Bell, Josephine, 75
Bernard, St, 28
Besant, Annie, 46-7, 99
Biblical criticism, 142
Birmingham Co-ordinating Committee for Coloured People, 72
Bisexuality, 121
Black, Clementina, 46
Blackstone, Sir William, 49
Book of Common Prayer, 92
Bossey, 61
Bradlaugh, 47, 99
British Association, 117
British Journal of Venereal Diseases, 72
Brown, W. Adams, 145
Brunner, Emil, 142, 144, 146-7
Bryant & May's, 46
Buber, Martin, 146
Buddhism, 103

Calvin, 40-3
Campbell-Bannerman, Sir Henry, 50
Canterbury, Archbishop of, 131
Catholic Marriage Manual, 58, 59
Cenchreae, 20
Champion, H. H., 46
China, 94, 95
Church of England Board for Social Responsibility, 128

Civil Service, 45
Clephane, Irene, 48
Clerical celibacy, 40
Cole, W. G., 2, 79
Concupiscence, 35, 40
Contraception, 99-115, 126-7
Co-operation, relevance of, 162-3
Cottage industries, 45-6
Creation, doctrine of, 143-51
Crime, 74, 78

Dante, 39
Darwin, 116
Deborah, 8
Decadence, 29
de Castro, Josué, 96, 97
Democracy, growth of, 45
Denning, Lord, 44
Divorce, 68-9
Docetism, 25
Domesticity, 54-5
Draft Convention on the Political Rights of Women, 53
Dualism, 11, 19-20, 37

Education, 49-50
Edward VIII, 5
Einstein, Albert, 118
Ellis, Havelock, 28
Equality before the law, 49

Fabian Society, 46
Fagley, Dr Richard M., 103, 115
Family Planning Association, 100
Femininity, 123-6
Feversham Committee, 88, 133
Finland, 52
Food and Agricultural Organization, 98
Francis, St, 39
Fulford, Roger, 53

Gifford Lectures, 152
Girton College, 50
Gladstone, Mr, 52
Gnosticism, 11, 26
Gorgonia, 38
Greeves, Frederic, 155-6
Gregory, St, 28
Gregory of Nyssa, 38
Ground-nut Scheme, 98

Healing, 165-6
Herbert Act, 1937, 68
Herod, 16

Herrenalb, 61
Hinduism, 103
Homosexuality, 9, 86-7, 121-2
Hunter, John, 131
Huxley, Julian, 83, 103
Huxley, T. H., 116

I and Thou, 146
Ibadan, 61
Iceland, 52
Illegitimacy, 70-2
Image of God, 146-7
India, 97, 129
Industrialization, 45-6
Infantile mortality, 96
Inge, Dean, 30, 50-1, 58
Innocent the Third, 39
Institute of Criminology, 74
Islam, 103

Japan, 97
Jenkins, Daniel, 57
Jerome, 18, 31
Jesus, 70, 148
   teaching on sexual relationship, 12-16
Joanna, 16
Joseph, 36, 149
Justin Martyr, 26
Jung, 152

Kelly, G. A., 127
Kinsey, Dr, 80-1
Klein, Viola, 6, 56, 123
Knox, 17
Knowlton pamphlet, 47

Ladies' Directory, 76
Lady Chatterley's Lover, 87
Lady Margaret Hall, 50
Lambeth Conference and Planned Parenthood, 108, 109
Lang, Archbishop, 5
Latourette, Professor, 38
Lawrence, D. H., 7, 87
Lecky, 80
Link, The, 46
London dock strike, 47
Luke, St, 16
Luther, 17, 40-3

Macarius, 28
Macaulay, 68
Macmillan, Harold, 88
Male headship, 20-3, 150-1

Malthus, 94, 102
Manichaeism, 27, 33
Marcion, 26
Marriage Guidance Movement, 2
Marriage as a remedy, 40, 41
   Jewish view of, 8
   Purposes of, 92
Married Women's Property Acts, 49
Mary Magdalene, 16
Mascall, Dr E. L., 150
Masculinity, 124-6
Masturbation, 120, 131
Matriarchy, 9
Matthew, Sir Tobie, 32
Mauritius, 94
Mead, Margaret, 123, 124
Medical Defence Union, 129
Methodist Statement on Planned Parenthood, 110-30
Migration, 98-9
Milk Marketing Board, 134
Mill, John Stuart, 45, 51
Ministry of Health, 72, 73
Ministry of Women, 22
Moffatt, Dr James, 24
Monasticism, 27-9
Monica, 34
Moore, Dr Barbara, 49
Moralism, 156-7, 166
Moral trends, 68-91
More, Hannah, 49

National Secular Society, 47
Naturalism, 6
New Zealand, 52
Niebuhr, Reinhold, 81, 142, 152
Nkongsamba, 61
N.S.P.C.C., 75

Obscene Publications Act, 87
One-sex Societies, 62, 63, 166-7
Orgasm, 79
Orwell, George, 134
Owen, Robert, 51

Pall Mall Gazette, 46
Pankhurst, Christabel, 51, 53
Pankhurst, Emmeline, 44, 50, 53
Paul, St, 5, 58, 66, 150-1
   attitude to sexual relationship, 16-23
Peru, 98
Pethick-Lawrence, Lord, 51, 161
Phoebe, 20
Pilgrim Fathers, 141
Pilkington Committee, 89-90

Pius XI, 105, 132
Pius XII, 105
Plato, 9
Plotinus, 33
Polycarp, 26
Population explosion, 92-115
Prior, 29
Prostitution, 46, 79-80
Protestant Churches and Planned Parenthood, 107-15
Protestant Reformation, 40-3
Providence, doctrine of, 135-9
Pusey, Dr, 47

Quadratus, 26

Rachael, 8
Radzinowicz, 74
Rathbone, Eleanor, 44
Reform Bill, 45
Renunciation, 27
Robinson, John, 141
Rollitt, Sir Albert, 52
Rolph, C. H., 103
Roman Catholic Church and Planned Parenthood, 104-7
R.S.P.C.A., 75
Russell, Sir E. John, 117, 138

Salpingectomy, 128
Salvation, doctrine of, 156-9
Science and religion, 116-19
Scientific humanism, 82-6
Scott, Sir Walter, 29
'Service of thinking', 163-4
Sex selection, 135
Sexual emancipation of women, 78-80
Sexuality, Greek attitude, 9-10
  Hebrew attitude, 6-8
  Oriental attitude, 10-12
  Roman attitude, 10

Significance of Material, 157
Simon Magus, 26
Sin of Adam and Eve, 7, 8
  doctrine of, 151-6
Skeptics, 33
Smith, Mr S., 52
Smith, Dr Kenneth, 102
Smyth, Dame Ethel, 44
Somerville College, 50
Stafford, Ann, 47
Status of Women, 1, 8, 12, 20-3, 44-67
Stead, W. T., 46
Sterilization, 127-30

Stopes, Dr Marie, 99-100
Street Offences Act, 76, 86
Summa Theologica, 39, 128
Susanna, 16
Symeon Stylites, 27
Syneisaktism, 37

Teenage spending, 89
Temple, William, 115
Tertullian, 18, 24, 29, 30, 31, 145
Therapeutae, 27
Thompson, William, 51
Theology, relevance of, 140-3
Tillich, Paul, 118, 142, 146
Timothy, 21
Trade Unions, 45, 46-8
Training, 164-5
Trevelyan, G. M., 45
Trinity, doctrine of, 145

United Nations, 53, 61
Universal Declaration of Human Rights, 53
U.S.S.R., 52

Valentinus, 26
Vasectomy, 129
Venereal diseases, 72-3
Victoria, Queen, 45, 59
Vidler, Alec R., 142
Virgin Birth, 15, 36, 40
Virgin Mary, 36

Walpole, Horace, 51
Wand, J. W. C., 25
Webb, Beatrice and Sidney, 47
Wesley, Charles, 155
Wesley Deaconesses, 64
Wesley, John, 63
Wesley, Susanna, 63
West, Dr D. J., 122
Widows, 20-1
Wilberforce, Bishop, 115
Wolfenden Report, 77, 80
Wolstonecraft, Mary, 51
Women in Parliament, 54
Women in the Ministry, 63-6, 167
Women's Suffrage Movement, 50-3
Woolf, Virginia, 54
Wootton, Baroness, 74, 83
Working wives, 55-7
Workman, H. B., 27
World Council of Churches, 2, 60, 101, 164

York, Archbishop of, 117

www.ingramcontent.com/pod-product-compliance
Lightning Source LLC
Chambersburg PA
CBHW050815160426
43192CB00010B/1763